ABCs *of* SPEAKING

"If you are an expert in your field (and if you aren't, either become one or find something you ARE an expert at!), you need to be on stage in front of people who can benefit from your expertise. In the ABCs of Speaking, Bret, Adryenn and Caterina provide you with a no-nonsense, get-to-the-point strategy guide that can help get you where you want to be! Be sure to read it A to Z."

— **Joel Comm**
New York Times Best-Selling Author of Twitter Power 2.0
JoelComm.com

"ABCs of Speaking is a must-read for anyone interested in making money, attracting clients, and delivering unforgettable speeches. Easy to read, each chapter is clear and concise, offering practical tips to develop your speaking career as a business, not just a hobby. In fact, I'm using Chapter B and its 10 key strategies to increase the number of bookings for my keynote speaking business. From A-to-Z, you'll find everything you need to get started and maximize your speaking experience."

— **Phil Johncock**, The Grant Professor
Award-Winning Author, Inspirational Speaker & Innovative Educator
PhilJohncock.com

"What an awesome resource for speakers! Save hours of time, lots of unnecessary aggravation and costly mistakes by referring to the 'ABCs of Speaking' before, during and after your next speaking engagement."

— **Ellyn Bader**
Director, The Couples Institute
CouplesInstitute.com

"To a great extent I've used speaking to help build Morgan James Publishing. Bret and the co-authors of his new book the ABCs of Speaking provide a wonderful introduction to the world of speaking for anyone looking to add speaking to their marketing mix. The content is clear and concise and I highly recommend it for any public speaker."

— **David Hancock**
Founder, Morgan James Publishing
MorganJamesPublishing.com

"Bret and the coauthors of this book are the definition of "Been There - Done That." Their experiences watching some of the best speakers in the world do well (and not so well) make this a book that should be on the shelf of anyone looking to take speaking seriously. The best training comes from experience—grab this now!"

— **Paul Colligan**
PaulColligan.com

"The ABCs of Speaking is a great primer for beginning speakers. This fast-reading book provides a cornucopia of hints for anyone who is looking to start a speaking business."

— **Wendy Lipton-Dibner**
3-time bestselling author and internationally recognized authority in business acceleration through transformational speaking
MovePeopleToAction.com

"A must have for aspiring and seasoned speakers.If you're looking for the A – Z of speaking, The ABCs of Speaking is the book to get. Each and every page is chock full of great insights on exactly what you need to do to secure speaking engagements and make money in the process. With everything from defining your ideal audience, putting your speaker sheet together, networking, self staged events, selling from the platform and more, this is a must have for anyone serious about their speaking career. Don't hesitate for a minute. Get a copy for you and anyone you know who aspires to be a well-paid speaker."

— **Kathleen Gage**
Award-winning Speaker, Author and Marketing Consultant
PowerUpForProfits.com

"In this practical guide to the speaking business, the authors have gifted us with a bucket full of gold nugget wisdom for burgeoning and experienced speakers. Not only do they share targeted key points on how to strengthen your speaking skills, they also give away the secrets on proven methods to put butts in the seats, work with promoters, and fulfill your passion to get your message out to the world. I especially enjoyed the chapter on storytelling and how to craft audience riveting talks from your own real life experiences. Well done! "

— **Dr. Dan Strakal**
International Award Winning Speaker,
Author, and Workplace Expert

"This is the book that every speaker would say 'I wish I had this before I made all of my costly mistakes!' The ABCs of Speaking is a true shortcut/checklist/manual for anyone intending to make a career of speaking from the stage. While it has great information on being an effective speaker, I believe its true gold is in providing precise guidance on the business side of speaking…the step-by-step information you ordinarily would have to learn the hard way. You can't go wrong with this speaker toolbox or handbook! Get this book and you are well on your way to igniting your life as a successful speaker. I'm recommending The ABCs of Speaking to all of my clients who are seeking to expand their speaking."

— **Jackie Lapin**
Founder, Conscious Media Relations
ConsciousMediaRelations.com

"In the ABCs of Speaking Adryenn, Bret, and Caterina have created a wonderful primer for those of us interested in developing speaking as a component of our businesses or making speaking our business focus. In this relatively short book (and easy read), they are at once comprehensive and specific, giving practical steps and advice in a wide range of topics that speakers, and aspiring speakers, need to know about. This is a reference that I know I will consult over and over again."

— **Mary Hiland, Ph.D.**
President, Hiland & Associates
Hiland-Assoc.com

"From soup to nuts, the alphabet soup for your speaking success. An instructional guide teaches you the essential ingredients you need to speak and win today".

— **Janet I Mueller**
JanetIMueller.com

"This book is brilliantly written and jam-packed with everything you need to know in order to succeed in the world of speaking. It has been said that the number one fear people have is public speaking. This book is without a doubt a must-have tool chest for new speakers and a magnificent reference for those already living in that space!"

— **Rose Sheehan**
Founder and CEO, Golden Egg Global
RoseSheehan360.com

ABCs

of SPEAKING

Your Building Blocks to Speaking Success

ADRYENN ASHLEY　　**BRET RIDGWAY**　　**CATERINA RANDO**

New York

ABCs of SPEAKING
Your Building Blocks to Speaking Success

Published in New York, New York, by Morgan James Publishing. Morgan James and The Entrepreneurial Publisher are trademarks of Morgan James, LLC. www.MorganJamesPublishing.com

The Morgan James Speakers Group can bring authors to your live event. For more information or to book an event visit The Morgan James Speakers Group at www.TheMorganJamesSpeakersGroup.com.

Shelfie

A **free** eBook edition is available with the purchase of this print book.

CLEARLY PRINT YOUR NAME ABOVE IN UPPER CASE

Instructions to claim your free eBook edition:
1. Download the Shelfie app for Android or iOS
2. Write your name in **UPPER CASE** above
3. Use the Shelfie app to submit a photo
4. Download your eBook to any device

ISBN 978-1-68350-012-4 paperback
ISBN 978-1-68350-013-1 eBook
Library of Congress Control Number: 2016904957

Cover Design by:
Rachel Lopez
www.r2cdesign.com

Interior Design by:
Bonnie Bushman
The Whole Caboodle Graphic Design

In an effort to support local communities, raise awareness and funds, Morgan James Publishing donates a percentage of all book sales for the life of each book to Habitat for Humanity Peninsula and Greater Williamsburg.

Get involved today! Visit
www.MorganJamesBuilds.com

TABLE OF CONTENTS

Chapter O Offers: Selling from the Stage   81
Chapter P Promoters   87
Chapter Q Quality vs. Quantity: Creating Your Criteria   93
Chapter R Responsibility   97
Chapter S Storytelling: How to Develop Stories to   103
           Be a More Compelling Speaker
Chapter T Technology: Friend and Foe   109
Chapter U Upsells and Under-valuing: How Much Money   117
           are You Leaving on the Table as a Speaker?
Chapter V Visibility: Social Media Strategies   123
Chapter W Writing a Book   129
Chapter X eXpanding Your Platform: Coaching,   135
           Membership Sites and Products
Chapter Y You: It's All About the Speaker… Or Is It?   141
Chapter Z ZZZZsss Avoid Them Nodding Off: 147
           Engage Your Audience and Be a Captivating
           Speaker Every Time

           About the Authors   153
           Additional Resources Available from Your Authors 157

ACKNOWLEDGMENTS

Adryenn Ashley

Here's to the crazy ones, the ones that would actually rather give the eulogy than be dead in a coffin. You are a rare breed, with a gift to be cultivated and grown. My coauthors and I wrote this book to shortcut your learning curve, to give you practical advice and steps to make certain that success was within your reach. It's your voice I long to hear, your message the world needs. So speak without hesitation and with the confidence that each step up on the platform can change lives for the better.

I also want to acknowledge my amazing coauthors, without whom this book would never have been born. To Bret, for always having my back and being an amazing friend—and for keeping this project alive to the end. To Caterina, for being a role model, mentor and friend. To Jesse and Sharla, for teaching me how to ask for the money without feeling like a hooker. To Sherry and Jodi, for your belief in me and my message, without which I never would have continued. To all of my amazing clients and members, you make the job worth it. Seeing you shine and grow and succeed is what keeps me going!

And, not least, my family, who supports me fully when I get to leave home to speak all over the world, even though they still don't quite understand what it is I do up on the stage. Thank you for your unconditional love.

Bret Ridgway

It's not often you have the opportunity to collaborate with two minds as brilliant as Adryenn Ashley and Caterina Rando and when I first conceived the idea for this book there was no question in my mind as to who I wanted to work with on this project. Now it was just coincidence that we had the ABCs covered—Adryenn being the "A", Bret being the "B" and Caterina the "C". My sincere thanks to both ladies for stepping forward and helping to create the outstanding work you have in your hands.

To our team at Speaker Fulfillment Services my on-going gratitude. Your dedication to keeping the needs of our clients first and foremost in your efforts is the key to our success. Your professionalism and "get it done" attitude is remarkable and I'm sure it's never said as often as it should be—"Thank you".

Finally, to my wife of 30+ years Karen for your unwavering support and love and to my children—Christina, Jacob and Mitchell. May you always strive to be of service to others so that you can truly succeed at the game of life. I'm so proud of all of you.

Caterina Rando

I am grateful to every person in every audience I have ever presented to, who sat attentively, smiling and nodding and sending me positive energy during the speech. I am truly grateful to you and everyone who encouraged me to get up and do my thing. I have found that there is nothing better than being yourself, sharing your value and being acknowledged for it. In other words, there is nothing better than speaking.

To Bret Ridgway who had the task of wrangling Adryenn and I to keep our wonderful book moving along, I thank you for your tenacity and commitment to this project. It is only because of you that we can now share our value and uplift others through this wonderful book.

To Adryenn Ashley who has been a bright light from the first day she welcomed me with open arms and and open heart to her Elite Speakers group. Thank you for your kindness and your friendship. You inspire me.

INTRODUCTION

The reason everyone is not using public speaking to grow their business is because most people are afraid of public speaking and, therefore, avoid it at all costs. If you like to speak or even if you are willing to speak, you will find it a highly effective way to attract new clients, build your email list and gain new opportunities. When you deliver a speech it is as if you are having an introductory phone call or an initial appointment with a whole room full of people all at once.

We could fill this book with all the reasons why you want to start to speak today. Suffice it to say here are some of the top reasons why you will want to read this book and take action immediately on what you read in the pages that follow.

The three of us who collaborated to put this book in your hands are all passionate about speaking—not only because we love to stand in front of an audience, but more importantly because we have gained hundreds of clients or earned in an afternoon what we might usually earn in a month from the privilege of doing so.

Here is what else we have gained from enjoying the spotlight of the platform. Here are the many reasons to get onboard the speaking bandwagon:

Become Recognized As an Expert In Your Field

When your name is on the event flyer and you are standing in the front of a room speaking on a topic, the audience members assume you are an expert on that topic. The more potential clients think you are an expert, the more likely they are to do business with you. You become known as an expert in your field, people will refer people to you when someone they know needs what you have to offer because being a speaker on a topic positions you as a sought after expert.

Meet More People Faster

People do business with people they know, like and trust. Speaking gives several people an opportunity to get to know you all at once. When anyone in your audience needs the services you provide, they will be more likely to call you because they have already met you and have begun to know you, like you and trust you because they received value from your presentation.

Educate Potential Clients

When you speak to promote your business, you have an opportunity to educate the audience about your industry and your business. People will know about the services you provide, what kinds of clients you work with, and what a client can expect from you. This can save you a lot of phone time and help you to pre-qualify people that are considering working with you.

Create New Opportunities

Speaking will allow you to go before groups of people that you may not otherwise meet. This can help you expand your sphere of influence, build your permission-based email list and provide you with a variety of new opportunities. The more people you deliver a speech to, the more opportunities for additional speeches, writing, and being a guest on radio and television shows will come your way.

Meet Other Experts and Leaders

Speaking allows you to meet other successful people in your industry. One day you may find yourself on the platform with the person you admire most. What could be better than that?

Always be gracious and generous with your time and acknowledge others for their accomplishments and their presentation. The other people you meet on the platform can be great referral sources and strategic alliance partners for you in your business.

More Clients, Contracts and Commissions

Speaking can be far more cost effective than advertising, direct mail, networking, or cold calling. The rate of return on the time investment you make to prepare for and deliver a speech could turn out to be the smartest action you could do to generate new business. If you have a strong delivery and give a high content speech, you could leave a speech with at least one new client every time you speak. Sometimes you could come home with ten or twenty new clients, which sure makes for a good day of speaking.

Increased Visibility

Whenever you are in the front of a room speaking to a group, you are being noticed. People will remember who you are and what your business does. The more people see you and see your business name, the more successful people think you are. Often, when you speak to a group, the group publicizes the event. Many people who do not attend the event will still read the information about your business and may give you a call. Even if people do not call you, know that the more people who read your name and see your picture the more they feel comfortable with you and begin to trust you for future business dealings.

Keeps You in Touch with the Public

Speaking keeps you in touch, and keeps you on your toes. It allows you to discover what issues are of concern to the people in your audiences. Then you can address these concerns in your articles, videos, blogs and on your website. Also, when you get out of your office and connect with new people they ask you questions or your opinion on topics you many have not yet thought to address. This can also result in new products, services and revenue streams for your company.

It is Good for Your Own Personal and Professional Growth

When you go to different groups, meetings and conferences as a guest speaker you will have many opportunities to hear other presenters on a variety of topics. Not only will this expand your network—you will learn a lot while keeping current on a variety of topics. This is always energizing and you may come home with an idea that will transform your business and uplift your life.

Perks, Perks and More Perks

As a guest speaker sometimes you are gifted nothing from the group that hosts you, sometimes you come home with a mug, a letter opener or a paperweight and sometimes you come home with beautiful flowers, dinner certificates and gift baskets. Also, once you get really known as a speaker you can be offered opportunities to speak on cruises, at fancy resorts, spas, even at exotic destinations all expenses paid.

Build a Better List, Better and Faster

When you go to speak to a group, the people in that group have a positive experience of you and you are beginning to build a relationship with them. When you do a drawing or offer them a discount if they give you their email address you are building your list. This is one of the key objectives you have as a business owner. You always want to be building your list.

The people on your list who have had a personal experience with you through your speech are more likely to do business with you sooner than someone who signs up and joins your email list through your website, but has never met you or seen you present.

More Money Later

Many people will be impressed with you when you speak and they may be interested in what you have to offer. They may not, however, be ready to hire you right now. By you staying in touch with them via email you will find that some people will come back to you later when they need what you have to offer.

Okay—that is enough of why speaking is so wonderful—get reading to figure out the how. When you do, so many good things will come to you.

The Coauthors of *The ABCs of Speaking,*
Adryenn Ashley, **B**ret Ridgway and **C**aterina Rando

Chapter A

ANALYSIS AND ACTION

You will find that a common theme throughout this book is that of making sure you treat your speaking career as a business rather than as a hobby. To that end, the need for you to continually analyze and research your market and your business to make sure you are getting the best results possible for the efforts you will be putting in is critical for your long-term success.

We will talk about some of these topics more in depth later in the book but here is a quick overview of some areas that we feel will require your detailed analysis to make sure you stay on track with your speaking business and continue to move things forward in a positive manner.

#1 What holes exist within the current market for which you would be a good fit? Where do your unique abilities and experiences best match up with a prospective audience that will want to hear your message? How can you tie your topic or topics into current events in some way that will make your expertise more "timely" than other alternatives out in the marketplace?

#2 What are the best ways for you to get the word out about your speaking and what you have to offer people? Online, offline, networking, direct mail, speakers bureaus, something else?

#3 What speaking model is the best fit for you? Fee or free? Or both? This is covered in depth in Chapter F of this book.

#4 How can you provide the audience you wish to serve with the optimal customer experience? Not only for the potential new customer possibly looking to book you as their next speaker, but also for your clients before and after an actual presentation.

#5 If you are selling from the platform what are your closing rates? What package or offer draws the best response, on average, from your audience? A physical product, coaching program, membership site, something else? And what price point gets the most responses? Various metrics are covered in detail in Chapter M.

#6 Amplification. How will you leverage your efforts best for long term gain? As your speaking business begins to grow how will you amplify your efforts to grow your business even faster? What tasks can you potentially outsource to others so that you can focus your efforts on more highly valued activities that only you can perform? What software or other resources can you incorporate into your daily operations that will speed up your progress?

Remember that we are looking at speaking as a business and not as a hobby. That means that you will need systems, processes and procedures developed and implemented for every aspect of your business to get things on track. Everything from how you get bookings, to making travel arrangements, to follow up communications with your clients, to product creation requires some level of standardization if you are going to build a business that is sustainable.

Your careful analysis as early in the game as possible as to what will make you stand out from the crowd in everything you do is so important. But, that being said, analysis without action is basically worthless. If you get yourself into a proverbial "Paralysis by Analysis" state then your speaking business will languish and you will not get the results that you want.

Imperfect Action is Better Than Perfect Analysis

It is often said that "Imperfect action is better than perfect analysis." Will you make mistakes along the way? Of course you will. But if you never make any mistakes then that means that you are not doing anything and that is far worse than making a mistake.

We have all run across brilliant people who seem to be plodding along, never achieving what they are fully capable of. In most cases, it is their inability to take action that holds them back. You have got to be an action taker to succeed as a speaker, even if that action is sometimes less than perfect.

I have seen a lot of great information products and a lot of great speakers never achieve the success they could have because someone insisted on crossing the same "t's" and dotting the same "i's" for the umpteenth time. There comes a time that good enough is good enough and you have got to put it out there—whether it is a new product or a new speech you want to present.

Bottom line, action trumps analysis almost every day of the week.

Chapter B

BOOKINGS, BOOKINGS, AND MORE BOOKINGS!

T he strategies to get booked shared with you here have allowed me to keep my calendar as full as I would like and, more importantly, have worked for my clients to go from no speeches to up to as many as eighty-seven speeches in one year.

Here are ten key strategies to getting booked. Follow them consistently and you will find many audiences full of gold:

1. Set Goals
I like to say a goal is a decision that has already been made. Decide how many talks you want to give, and in what time frame. Set a monthly, quarterly and annual goal. There are many ways you can reach your goals. You can host your own events, do teleclasses and webinars and you can also partner with other service providers and put together a workshop.

After your goals are set, put together your schedule for when you are going to focus on getting booked. I recommend three hours a week. You can also have your assistant work on this for you if you are not getting to it. When you consistently devote three hours a week to getting booked you will find the opportunities will be rolling in.

2. Get Your Speaker Sheet Done

Your speaker sheet is what gets you booked as a speaker. It is a PDF® that has been well designed to match your brand. It will include your picture or pictures of you speaking and describe your speaking style (energetic, warm, dynamic) and your talks (uplifting, innovative, thought-provoking). List a max of three of your most popular speeches, you do not want to share too many. You also want to be loud and proud about the value your talk delivers. Describe the benefits of your talk and what insights your audience will discover.

Be sure to include a list of places where you have spoken, plus testimonials from the meeting planners. Also, do not forget your contact information. If you are just getting started and do not have all this information, do it anyway. The beauty of today's technology means you do not have to print your speaker sheet. You can always update it after every talk and just email the PDF file.

Simply having a well put together speaker sheet can get you booked many times over. One of my clients, Vicki, a construction industry expert was just getting started speaking and sent in her speaker sheet to present at a conference. She was the only one with a marketing piece just for speaking. All the other people sent in their brochures. Yes, they looked like experts but not speakers. Vicki got the gig and is now the most sought after speaker in her industry.

3. Be Loud and Proud About the Value You Bring

Let's get the word out. On your website, make sure you tell people you are a speaker. Make it part of your business description in your social media profiles. Add a speaker page—that's where you include your speaker bio, talk topics and a link to your speaker sheet. Use social media to tell people about the talks you give, ask your contacts for ideas on where you can give a speech, and announce the places where you have been booked. Be sure to invite your contacts to come hear you speak! Make sure you send an announcement to your email list, and ask them to forward it on to anyone else who might be interested.

Always be sure to mention the topic you are presenting on when you mention you got a booking or gave a speech through social media. One of my clients, Dortha, an online marketing manager, posted on her Facebook® page that she was looking to give her business building talk to more groups and in thirty minutes she got eight bookings. It is time for you to be loud and proud that you are a speaker.

4. Ask for Referrals

Start with your immediate community. Ask your clients, friends and colleagues what groups they belong to. Ask them to provide you with a contact. These warm leads will always be the best way to get booked. Next, brainstorm with the people you know what groups they know of where you would like to speak. Depending on your topic this can include church groups, PTA meetings, professional associations and private clubs. Consider medical and law enforcement associations as well as neighborhood groups. Also, check newspapers for meeting announcements and Internet event calendars for groups in your area.

5. Do Research and Build a List

Once you build your basic list, it is time to go online. Start with a Google search for *type of group* + *local area* + *the year*. For example: *image consultant* + *San Jose* + *2017*. Add in the word *organization* or *association* for a more refined search. Follow the listings to the different websites. Note when they have their meetings and who the contact person is. You will usually want to contact the program chair, education chair, meeting chair or president.

With all this research, one caveat: Make sure your ideal potential clients are at these events. Do not chase bookings for the practice or experience. Your goal is to connect with the people who will be interested in hiring you.

6. Reach Out to Groups

Once you know how to contact, reach out to that person and offer your services as a speaker. Emailing the first time is fine because you can attach your speaker sheet. If you do not get a response in few days, follow up with a phone call.

7. Follow Up, Follow Up Follow Up

Be aware that most groups are run by volunteers and often change leadership every year. This means it can take a bit of detective work to make certain you are contacting the right person, and it might take some time before someone gets back to you. Your best bet is a personal contact who can point you in the right direction and also vouch for you as a speaker. If you can get someone from their group, association or company to come hear you speak, please do. They will be much more likely to book you after they have heard you.

8. When You Speak Ask for More Speeches

This is another important aspect about being loud and proud. When you finish your talk, ask if anyone in the audience knows of another group that might like to hear you speak. This is a great way to keep building your list. One of my clients, Karen, an etiquette consultant, booked nineteen speeches in a short period of time simply by asking her audiences for other places for her to speak.

9. Be an Awesome Speaker and People Will Ask You to Speak

There is no getting around it. The better speaker you are the more clients you will come home with and the more bookings will fall in your lap. Work on your speaking skills as much as you work on any other business skill.

To Master the Art of Speaking Practice,
Practice, Practice in Front of
Real Live Audiences

To master the art of speaking, practice, practice, practice in front of real live audiences. The more you do it, the easier it gets. First, you get to ease, then you move toward mastery. Rosie, a productivity expert had never given a speech for business when we met. She quickly booked twenty-two speeches in six months and reported with glee that each one was easier than the last one. You can expect the same result.

10. Create Your Own Speaking Opportunities

You can create your own speaking opportunities. This is one of the best, fastest ways to build your business, become a masterful speaker and come home with clients. It's your party, your event. Webinars, teleseminars and live, in-person programs are great ways to connect with your target audience. Holding your own events continues to build your reputation, influence and reach. Linda, a feng shui master had been presenting for twenty years. It was only after she started doing her own events that her client base, her reputation and her bottom line swelled. I see this often. Do not wait to do your own events.

Follow these ideas here and soon you will find that both your calendar and your bank account are full and you are wearing a huge smile each day.

Chapter C

CONTENT
What Are You Going to Teach Them?

There is no question that as a speaker there are any number of different factors you have to consider when you are thinking about the topic on which you want to speak. If you are speaking as a means of establishing yourself as an expert to generate leads for your core product or service then your presentation may be vastly different than if being a professional speaker is your core business.

You have obviously gained a lot of experience over the course of your career and, while many recommend you have multiple speeches you can deliver, most encourage you have one "go to" speech that is what you are primarily known for.

But what should your "go to" speech be about? If you really want to position yourself as the expert in your market then it is critical you understand that it must be about much more then simply picking a niche.

The best explanation I ever heard about this was from Rich Schefren of StrategicProfits.com. Rich wrote an article a while back for the No B.S.™ Marketing Letter titled *"How to Find Your Own Sweet Spot in Your Marketplace."* In his article Rich talked about how many entrepreneurs fail because they go out in search of a niche rather than a sweet spot.

I would contend that the same exact conclusion can be drawn for speakers

---

According to Rich this is because a niche is solely based on external factors, like a recognized need or a problem in need of a solution. In stark contrast, a sweet spot is based on your own internal factors—such as your strengths, talents, experiences, passions, and so on.

So, what is your "sweet spot" as a speaker? Rich believes that everyone has a sweet spot, but it can take a significant amount of research and introspection on your part to find it. But, it will be well worth the effort.

Your sweet spot is that unique advantage that you have in the marketplace and, once you find it, Rich says that it makes your marketing 100x easier once you can articulate your sweet spot.

Rich offered a helpful exercise that can possible help you find your own sweet spot.

First, get out your journal, and make three lists.

1. Start by thinking about what you're passionate about. Ask yourself:
   - What excites you?
   - What motivates you?
   - What conversations do you feel you must take part in?
   - What gets you out of bed in the morning?

2. Then move on to your strengths:
   • What have you always been good at?
   • What have you used to make a living up to now?
   • What do your friends and family say are your best strengths?
   • Do you already have an area of your life where your friends regularly ask for your advice?
   • Do you have any advice you often give that's not common knowledge?
3. Then look at your past:
   • What unique experiences have you had?
   • How have past experiences made you who you are today?
   • Any great stories you always tell?

Once you have all of this written down look at your lists. If there is any crossover between the lists where your passions, strengths, and experience meet up then that is a good place to start looking for your sweet spot in the market.

Maybe you have already determined your sweet spot and know what your "go to" topic is. If so, great and congratulations. But, even after you have answered these questions, there are several other factors related to your content to which you will need to give consideration. This includes questions like:

• Are you going to customize each presentation for your audience?
• What will your teaching style be?
• Will you incorporate humor and/or storytelling into your presentations?
• Can you somehow tie in current events to your presentations to make your topic more timely to prospective clients?
• If you are speaking at a multi-speaker event what are the other speakers talking about?

Let's take a look at each of these questions.

Customization

A common question you should anticipate from prospective clients who are considering you for some type of keynote presentation is "Will you customize your presentation for my audience?" The answer should always be "Yes".

Will it mean a bit more work on your end? You bet. But the benefits of customizing your presentation to your audience are significant. First, by demonstrating that you are responsive to the requests of your client you will be regarded much more highly and dramatically increase your chances of landing additional speaking engagements with that client.

And word gets around. When you become known as one of those people that are easy to work with and will go the extra mile for their clients then more and more work will come your way.

Second, when you take the time to truly understand the wants and needs of your audience and know the demographics of your crowd then you will be able to craft a much more impactful speech. Ever heard the expression "I felt like he was talking right to me"? When your audience has that reaction you will find them much more receptive to your message and, if appropriate, to your product offerings.

Teaching Style

Are you a "gung-ho take no prisoners" kind of person or a more laid back "just telling some stories" kind of person? There is no right or wrong answer here. Maybe you are somewhere in between. Regardless of what your personality style is, your teaching style will probably be reflective of your personality.

We talk elsewhere in this book about the need to be "authentic". It applies fully to your teaching style. If you try to be something you are not then more than likely it will catch up with you eventually and your success will wane because you are not being true to yourself.

Regardless of which side of the fence you fall on you can significantly increase your success on stage by more actively involving your audience in your presentation. We will talk in a later chapter about "controlling your environment" but for now let us stick to the general topic of "interactivity". The question for you is "How will you get your audience to interact with you in a manner you can control?"

Many do it by asking questions to which they already know the answer. Others informally survey the room to get people to raise their hand, while others get their audience involved with more detailed hands-on experiences. Again, no right or wrong answer here. Just the question of what will you do to get your audience involved in your presentation.

Use Humor With Great Caution

Humor/Storytelling

A large part of many speakers teaching style is their use of humor and/or storytelling in their presentation. People generally love stories and if you can call upon your life experiences for a story that helps you to illustrate a point you should take full advantage of that story.

Humor can be great also but one must use humor with great caution. What is funny to you may not be funny to another. You should generally be politically correct and avoid talking about powder keg subjects like religion and politics.

Current Events

The ability to relate any part of your presentation to the current events of the day is another great way to better relate to your audience. When they see that your content is "fresh" and is related to things they are hearing about in the news this makes your topic more attractive and timely for them.

Meeting planners typically schedule their speakers well in advance so this is a little trickier to do when you are trying to attract future speaking engagements. But the customization we spoke of earlier can also include current events and your ability to make your presentation more "trendy" can help establish long term relationships in the industry.

Multi-Speaker Events

If you are speaking at an event that will have multiple speakers across a few day period it is so important that you try to find in advance what each of the other speakers will be talking about.

Let me tell you a story (See, storytelling works great in books also).

A few years ago I was attending an Internet marketing conference that featured somewhere around 18-20 total speakers over the course of the three day event. The event promoter had selected his speakers based upon name value alone. No thought was given whatsoever (or so it seemed) to what topic each speaker would be presenting.

So, what happened? As it turned out there were three different speakers at this same event talking about the subject of copywriting. So, by the time the third speaker got up to do his presentation the audience was already bored with the subject of copywriting. And when that speaker tried to sell his copywriting products/services at the end of his presentation the audience had already heard two other offers related to copywriting. Bottom line—he bombed!

If he would have found out in advance that two others on the stage before him were talking about copywriting also he would at least have had the opportunity to change his presentation in some way to make it different than the others. But he did not know in advance and was not able to adapt on the fly so his results were not nearly what he wanted.

Chapter D

DEMOGRAPHICS
Knowing Your Audience

W ithout question one of the major contributors to the successful delivery of a speech is to have your audience all feel as if you are talking directly to them. The ability to connect at a "heart level" greatly increases the bond you have with your audience and leads to a well-received presentation.

Connect With Your Audience
At a Heart Level

It does not matter if your speech is a keynote presentation or a platform selling situation. If you understand the demographics of your audience then you can better tailor your content in order to connect at a deeper level with the crowd.

So what types of information would you want to know in advance of a presentation about the audience that might help you do a better job? This list is not necessarily all-inclusive, but is a good starting point for you.

- Is your audience primarily male or female?
- What is the average age of the audience? Are you talking to teens, baby boomers, senior citizens, etc.?
- Where are the audience attendees from? Is it a local crowd, a regional gathering, national or international?
- What is their educational background?
- What type(s) of businesses are represented in the audience? (For example, you would not want to use a bunch of real estate examples if you are talking with a group of restaurant owners)
- Is it a G—PG—PG13—R—or "F Bomb" type of crowd?
- Have you delivered a presentation to this same audience previously?
- If it is a multiple speaker event, who else is sharing the platform and what will they be talking about?

Much of this information should be available from the event promoter. Large events that have been held many times in the past also often have sponsorship packets that contain great demographic information about the attendees because they are trying to attract sponsorship money. But you can use this information also to learn more about the audience to which you will be speaking.

If you are delivering a keynote presentation, particularly to a single corporate client then you will want to do some research to try to figure out who the "movers and shakers" are within the audience. A great way to find this information is to simply call the main switchboard of the company for which you will be presenting. Explain you are delivering a keynote for them at their upcoming event and ask the gatekeeper about the key people who will be attending.

You would be amazed at the kind of information you can gather that will enable you to craft your presentation specifically for that company. When you have the ability to acknowledge key people in the audience during the course of your presentation you really can connect at a much deeper level.

Remember, the more that you can address the specific pain point(s) of the group you will be speaking to the more receptive your audience will be to your presentation. When they feel that you are talking directly to them you come across as much more professional because you have taken the time to truly understand their needs and to deliver information that will be of benefit to them.

And it does not matter if it is a keynote presentation or a platform selling situation. The "pain points" are the critical elements you must incorporate into your presentation. More specifically, your solution for those pain points is what will truly ingratiate you with your audience.

Do not hesitate to do some keyword research in advance of an event to try to find out what the questions are that are being asked online related to your topic. The more you can tie in the current things people are looking for solutions for to your presentation the better you will do.

Now, in a platform selling situation there are some additional pieces of information you will want to try to gather in advance that can greatly increase your chances of increasing your back of the room sales. You will want to ask the event promoter these questions, but do not take the word of the promoter as "gospel."

If you are speaking at an event that has been held previously you will want to find out who has spoken at the event previously and at what price point their offer was. Ask the promoter what was the price point of the speaker that had the most success at their last event and on what topic did they speak? In general, what price point gets the most action for that promoter's events? If you come in with a $2000 offer and the crowd has only been exposed to $500 price points in the past you, in most cases, greatly decrease your chances for success.

Admittedly, sometimes it is difficult to get this information from the promoter. But if you explain you want to do the best job possible for them at the event they will usually understand and be as forthcoming as possible.

Another great source of information about what worked and did not work at previous events is from those people that provided testimonials for the last event. If you look at the promotional website for the upcoming event you will typically find testimonials from previous attendees. It is pretty easy to find these people online and ask them some questions about the event.

Also, once you have been around the speaker circuit for a while you will have speaking colleagues you have built a trust relationship with that are willing to share their experiences with you about working with different promoters.

If you have a contract with an event promoter for an upcoming event (and you always should) then you will want to, if at all possible, incorporate some language into that contract that allows you the ability to adjust your offer and price point at the event if you see certain things are not working with other speakers. A reasonable promoter will be willing to work with you because they have a vested interest in your success also.

Knowing as much about your audience as possible before delivering a presentation seems like a no-brainer. But, you would be surprised at the number of speakers who are unwilling to take the time to get to know their audience in advance so they can fine tune their presentation for that audience.

Does it take a little bit of work? Of course it does. But there may be some aspects of your audience marketing research that you can enlist the assistance of a support person to help you with. Whether you do it all yourself or whether someone helps you, the time invested in getting to know your upcoming audiences better will pay massive dividends for you over the long haul.

People definitely buy from those that they know, like and trust. And whether it is simply "buying" your message or whether it is about buying your product, your ability to craft a presentation that is laser-focused to the needs of your audience can only be done if you really know your audience well. And when you do that your know, like and trust factor can grow exponentially.

Chapter E

ENVIRONMENT
Controlling the Room

To maximize your effectiveness as a speaker it is of paramount importance that you control the environment in which you will be speaking as much as possible. Your environment can certainly include things like the room temperature and lighting. But it will also include a lot of other factors you may not have considered previously.

Anything that can influence your onstage performance falls under the classification of your environment. Some may be considered major and others minor, but all can affect how well your message is received by the audience and, if you are selling from the platform, how well you sell.

We are talking about things like:

- Sound quality
- Your introduction
- Internet connections
- Clicker

- Banging doors
- Q & A sessions
- Testimonials from the audience
- Intro and exit music

Sound Quality

I have seen too many speakers show up too close to the scheduled start of their presentation. So the audio crew is slapping a microphone on them at the last minute and there is not enough time to do a proper sound check prior to the speaker taking stage. And then they wonder why the audio quality sucks during their presentation.

That is why you should get to an event well in advance of any scheduled presentation. If you speak before lunch find out when the audio crew will be in the room either the night before or the morning of your scheduled presentation so a proper sound check can be done. If you speak after lunch then check things out during the lunch break. Find out specifically where on your clothing you should affix the microphone for best sound.

Also, walk the stage when you are mic'ed up to check for spots you should avoid walking during your presentation. Spots where interference is caused and the audience would get a loud "shriek" or other earsplitting sound that will detract from your presentation. Know the "hot spots" going in and you will have a better sounding presentation throughout your speech.

Your Introduction

Should you pre-write the introduction you want the event emcee or whoever will be introducing you to the audience to read? In a word—yes. Does that mean every person who does your intro over the course of your speaking career will read it word for word? Of course not. But if you do not have something for the emcee to follow and they "wing" it who knows what you are going to get. So write something out and get it to the proper person enough in advance so they can at least familiarize themselves with what they will be saying about you.

If you have a colleague at an event who has done a great job of introducing you at a previous event then the event promoter may let that person do your intro rather than the event emcee. If the audience already knows, likes and trusts your colleague that can be a fantastic idea. But if your colleague is someone they won't be familiar with you are better off utilizing the event emcee.

Regardless of who will be doing your intro, do NOT make it a complete autobiography. I have seen many speakers lose their audience before they ever uttered their first word on stage. How? With an introduction that went on and on and on and on and on. You get the idea. Many speakers think they need to credentialize themselves on stage much more then they need to. The audience is interested in what is in it for them and the minutes on how wonderful you are and the great things you've done just does not do it for them. The fact that you are on the stage in the first place pretty much provides you with all the credentials you need.

The Fact that You Are on Stage Provides
You With Important Credentials

And, if I hear another speaker say "I don't say this to impress you, but rather to impress upon you..." then I might be sick. A two to three minute introduction should be satisfactory and the primary focus should be on what your audience is going to learn, not on how great you are. Some speakers have gone to video introductions to exercise maximum control over their introductions. You will have to decide if this is right for you.

Internet Connection

Never ever ever ever do a presentation where you are relying on a live Internet connection to show something to the audience. This is one of those things in your environment that you have very little control over. I have seen too many presentations ruined by a lost or a very slow Internet connection. You are taking an unnecessary chance anytime you try to go live online.

The way you control this factor is to use screen shots from the web in your presentation rather then the live shot. It works as well and you don't run the risk of looking the fool with connectivity issues. Internet connections in meeting rooms can also be very expensive—hundreds of dollars per day. So you may also be asking the event promoter to incur an additional expense just for you that could have been avoided.

Clicker

Another seemingly minor factor that can cause you major headaches is the simple clicker. If you are utilizing a PowerPoint in your presentation then in all likelihood you will be controlling your PowerPoint with a wireless clicker. Be sure to test the clicker in advance of your presentation so you understand fully its range and exactly where you should point it when you are ready to advance to your next slide.

Banging Doors

A smart event promoter tries to control audience access to the meeting room through a pre-selected set of doors. They do this for several reasons. One reason is that it gives them the ability to do a better job of greeting their audience by knowing what doors they will be entering the meeting room through. Another reason is it enables them to force the crowd to pass by the sales table whenever they are exiting the room.

During your presentation people will invariably be coming in or going out of the room and if the door bangs noisily shut every time someone passes through it can be a major distraction to the participants. You want them focusing their attention on you and not turning to look and see who is coming in or going out every time they hear the door.

There are a couple of low tech solutions you can suggest to an event promoter if you see that the doors could be a problem. First, you can suggest they tape the push bar of the exit door(s) shut. This does not hinder exit access in any way but does silence the noisy push bar that people hear when the door is being opened.

But then the door closes, sometimes with a loud bang. So the second thing you can suggest is simply throwing a towel over the top of the door to cushion things when the door shuts. Simply eliminating these two potential distractions can help you to better control your environment.

Q & A Sessions

Should you take questions during your presentation? In all but rare cases I would say no. Turning control of the microphone over to someone in the audience is the quickest way to lose control of your presentation. Invite them to meet you at the sales table if they have any questions or to come and talk with you during a break.

You should already have a sense of what questions people will ask you about your topic and you should have the answers to the questions you are most frequently asked already worked into your presentation.

Testimonials from the Audience

Like Q & A sessions, soliciting testimonials from the audience about your products or services is an area fraught with potential problems. First, you must alert the event promoter ahead of time if you will have need of a microphone in the audience at some point in your presentation. Otherwise, you can have a few awkward moments of silence while they are scrambling around for a microphone.

Even if you have made all the arrangements in advance you are still turning over control of your room to someone else when you give them a microphone. Just like we spoke of introductions that can go on and on I have also seen testimonials get totally out of control and last way too long. Sometimes it is hard to wrest back control of the microphone.

If you are going to use live testimonials you must carefully chose who you are going to use. Give them clear guidelines on how much time they will have when you go to them for their testimonial and make sure you know what they are going to be saying ahead of time so you don't get any unexpected surprises.

Intro and Exit Music

Music can have a powerful impact on people. Properly selected music played as you are getting ready to take the stage or when you have just finished and are exiting the stage can help you to create some real excitement in the room. You can help by selecting music you feel best fits with your presentation. A smart promoter will be more then happy to accommodate your musical requests.

In Conclusion

While there are some factors in your environment you may have little or no control over, such as the room temperature and event lighting, you can see there are a number of other factors you may exercise some control over. Remember, the better you control your overall speaking "environment" the better are your chances for success.

Chapter F

FEE OR FREE
Speaking Models

W hy do you want to become a speaker? Is it because you have a powerful message you want to share with the world? Or, maybe because you recognize that being the one in the front of the room providing training or information automatically establishes you as an "expert?" Maybe you just like being the center of attention.

Whatever your reason there is no doubt that being a speaker can establish you as an expert and as someone to which people should pay attention. Even if you don't want to be a full-time professional speaker we have already talked in the introduction about all the awesome reasons to become a speaker.

Speaking for Local Organizations
If you are speaking primarily to establish yourself as an expert in order to directly or indirectly promote your primary products or services then

chances are most of your speaking engagements will be of the free variety. If you are speaking for local organizations like Chambers of Commerce, Rotary Club or others then your time in front of the room will be non-compensated time and you probably won't be able to make any direct sales at the actual event.

And there is nothing wrong with this type of speaking. It is a marketing tool for your organization and through careful tracking of where your new business comes from you will be able to tell whether the speaking that you are doing is proving profitable or not. I frequently deliver content-only sessions for various conferences simply for the sharing of information I know will help the audience and will establish me as the expert.

Getting "Paid" Even When Speaking for Free

Even if you are a non-compensated speaker there may be other ways you can be "paid" by the organizations you speak for. Here are a few other ways to get paid when speaking for free from Bryan Caplovitz of SpeakerMatch.com

- Ask for a professional quality video of your presentation
- Have them buy your product (book, CD, resource kit) instead.
- Request a testimonial on the organization's letterhead
- Ask for a write-up in the organization's newsletter
- Use business cards to your advantage
- Use your audience as a source for leads
- Get a professional photo shoot showing audience reaction

If you are going to opt to take on speaking as your full-time profession you are going to have to determine which speaking model you want to pursue. Neither is mutually exclusive and you may end up with a hybrid model over time. But, it is important to understand the primary two models when you are getting started, which we will call "Fee" and "Free".

The For "Fee" Speaking Model

In the "Fee" speaking model you are paid a pre-determined amount by an event promoter to come and speak at their event. This fee can range anywhere from literally nothing when you are starting out and just trying to gain experience up to the tens of thousands of dollars or more when you reach the big time. Commonly known as "Keynote" speakers, there are thousands of people worldwide who make their full-time living delivering keynote presentations for corporations, associations and other groups.

The big-name celebrity speakers that command fees in the hundreds of thousands of dollars, or more, are usually celebrities first and speakers second. Donald Trump, Bill Clinton and Colin Powell are great speaking role models we can all strive to emulate, but know that they are the exception rather then the rule when it comes to fees. But do dream big.

As a for "Fee" or "Keynote" speaker your speaking income is your speaking fee primarily and your speaking fee alone. Typically, the event promoter will also cover your travel expenses including airfare, transportation to and from the hotel, lodging and meals. Your individual negotiating skills will determine what above and beyond the norm you are able to get.

If you have a book or other relevant materials you may be able to get the promoter to agree to purchase one for every attendee at the event. So even though you may not be allowed to sell from the platform you may have the opportunity to generate a little extra income from book sales. Again, how good of a negotiator are you?

Be sure to study other speakers in your area of expertise to get a feel for what they are charging for similar speeches. You will find most have a range of fees depending upon the topic and other factors. You need to decide if you are going to compete on the basis of price (not recommended) or quality. Make sure you have an outstanding value proposition for any event promoter for whatever fee level you decide on.

The For "Free" Speaking Model

There is a second kind of speaker, called the "Free" speaker and if you are able to sell effectively from the platform then this is the speaking model you may want to follow. In the "free" model a speaker is brought in by an event promoter to speak to their audience for no up front compensation.

In this model your compensation comes in the form of a split of the product sales you make at the event. You pay your own travel expenses usually and both the promoter and you are gambling, in a sense, that you will sell enough from the stage to make the time you are given in front of the audience profitable for both yourself and the promoter.

Most of the events of this type are multiple speaker events lasting anywhere from two to four days. So you are usually competing with many other speakers over the course of the event for a share of the wallets of those in the audience. But, if you bring real value to an audience and you have an outstanding offer for continuing education, products or services then you can make significantly more money as a "Free" speaker then you can as a "Fee" speaker.

I have a colleague who has sold as high as $995,000 in products from the platform at a single event. Even keeping in mind that the traditional split of the sales you make at an event is 50/50 with the event promoter, in this case my colleague pocketed a mere $447,500 for one ninety minute presentation. Not too shabby!

You Can Make Significantly More Money as a
"Free" Speaker Then You Can as a "Fee" Speaker

Some promoters offer different splits so always be sure to carefully read any speaker contract before you sign it to make sure you fully understand the terms and conditions associated with working with a particular event promoter. I have seen some cases where the back of the room sales split was 60/40 or even 70/30 in favor of the promoter so be aware.

In a typical 50/50 split the norm in the industry is to have the credit card transaction fees for orders absorbed by the promoter and the hard product costs associated with fulfillment of the sale borne by the speaker. But again, this is another detail of which you should be aware in advance so there are no misunderstandings with a promoter.

There are some rare cases where an event promoter that is paying you a fee to speak may also allow product sales in the back of the room. And I have seen scenarios where a non-savvy promoter has allowed the speaker to have 100% of their back of the room sales in addition to the speaking fee they received. Again, this is rare but always nice to have happen.

Fee or Free? It can be a tough decision for many speakers and you will have to decide which model fits you if you want to be a full-time professional speaker. The real money for the speaker who can sell effectively is in the "Free" model. But the burden is on you to sell to be paid and that may or may not be consistent with your personality and mindset.

Chapter G

GETTING THE WORD OUT
Your Speaker Sheet

As we have discussed, speaking is an excellent way to showcase your expertise, meet people, get clients and even get paid just for your speech. In order to get speaking engagements, you first need to get booked and that means you need a speaker sheet. A speaker sheet is a PDF® or electronic document that is your marketing brochure to get you booked as a speaker.

If you are a new speaker start with a one-page document. If you have been speaking for a while you may want to go to two pages. This speaker sheet can be downloaded from your website and you will send it out via email to people you want to book you for speaking.

You may want to have some printed on high quality paper to send out for higher-end bookings or to have available at your events when someone says they would like to book you.

---

*If You are a Professional Speaker
Your Speaker Sheet Will be a Key to
Even be Considered for a Booking*

If you are a professional speaker your speaker sheet will be a key to even be considered for a booking. If you are a speaker who uses speaking for marketing having a speaker sheet will get you booked time and time again over other people. Other people who do what you do and say they speak but do not have a speaker sheet. This will differentiate you from every other consultant who says they want to speak. This is key.

Decide what you are going to talk about and choose a topic that interests the groups where your potential strategic alliances gather. For example, if you want strategic alliances for women in leadership, you could do a talk on Five Secrets for Chairing the Perfect Board Meeting.

What to include in your speaker sheet.
✓ **Catchy benefit-focused title at the top of the page**

Start your speaker sheet with a catchy phrase or a phrase that clearly captures the benefit of your speech. Emphasize what audience members will get. Here are three examples of titles clients of mine use on their speaker sheets: "Becoming Great with Money", "How to Add an Hour of Productivity Every Day" or "How to Look Like a Million Dollars on a Budget."

Here is the big rookie mistake I see all the time. People put their names in huge letters at the top of their speaker sheet. I guess they are thinking of a Broadway show marquee, because we all have a desire to see our name in lights. However, most of us are not yet a household name and your name is not enough to captivate the meeting planner and catch his or her attention. That is why you go with a benefit-focused title.

✓ **Professional photo**

Invest in a professional photo session. It is okay to do a little touch up, but do not overdo it as you still want to look like your picture. You want a photo you love and are thrilled to put out there. If you have action shots then even better, use one of these if you are doing a two paged speaker sheet. And remember to update your picture on a fairly regular basis. Nothing turns off someone more than a speaker picture that was clearly taken twenty years ago. Make sure any photos you include on your speaker sheet are a minimum of 300 dpi resolution if you are going to print them. Lower resolution photos are fine for online (72 dpi typically), but not suitable for print purposes.

✓ **Bio that describes you as a speaker**

In addition to your credentials, make sure you include a couple of sentences about your presentation style. For example, 'Sheila is a dynamic and high-energy presenter who provides an interactive program that keeps the audience engaged.' Or 'David is a down-to-earth presenter who makes tech-speak easy to understand and gives audiences ideas they can apply immediately to improve marketing online.' This is another key aspect to your speaker sheet that is often overlooked. The purpose of your speaker sheet is only to get you booked. Be sure the language of it describes your speaking style and how the audience will react.

✓ **List the titles of your talks**

A list of topics you speak on and the benefits of each topic. Start with no more than three. One or two titles are fine also. Too many speeches on your sheet is another beginner mistake. If you are a professional speaker who has been presenting for quite a while then having more topics is fine. Be sure that your talks match your branding, products and services. This way when you make an offer or ever let people know they can purchase your book, the title of your book is the same as the title of your talk.

✓ **Paragraph descriptions or bullet point descriptions**

Underneath each title discuss the benefits audience members will receive by listening to your talk. Tell them not what you are going to discuss but instead the value audience members will take away from what you have discussed. Make sure your language is clear and specific on what they will take away. This will help you get booked more.

✓ **A list of speaking clients (if you have them)**

List the names or companies, associations and organizations you have spoken for before. Make sure they match the kinds of organizations you want to book you. For example, if your aim is to get booked at major corporations do not include the churches or community organizations you presented to. If you want to speak to more churches and community groups then you would create a different speaker sheet for that.

✓ **Up to six testimonials from groups you have spoken to (if you have them.)**

After you do a talk ask your contact for a statement describing what a great job you did and how valuable your talk was for the group. With the testimonial be sure to include their name and organization or company.

We want the speaker booker to think that you are a great match for their group. That is why the same instruction applies here as we mentioned for the client list. Only include testimonials from organizations like the places you want to get booked. For example, on my speaker sheet to get booked to speak at business women's conferences I only have testimonials from other business women's conferences.

Another challenge I see with new speakers is that they include participant or audience member testimonials. That is not what you want here. Those you would use for a public seminar that people sign up for individually. Stick with the program chairs, presidents, conference organizers for your speaker sheet testimonials.

✓ **Your contact information at the bottom of the page**
List your email, website and phone on the bottom of the sheet so you can easily be contacted.

✓ **Be sure to get a professional design**
I see so many speaker sheets that are well written however they have been sent out to bookers without the benefit of a professional design. Make sure you invest a little money to make your speaker sheet look great and be consistent with your branding. You want to make sure you look like an experienced, professional speaker. Without a professional design that does not happen.

In addition to your speaker sheet, you also want a speaker page on your website to position you as a speaker, which is key if you want people to call you to speak. This would look just like your speaker sheet only be a page on your site that potential bookers can go through. Do have your speaker sheet on this page for downloading.

Follow these key elements to get your speaker sheet done. Once that happens you are ready to get booked. Put together your list of organizations to contact and send an email out with your speaker sheet attached and watch yourself get booked over and over.

Chapter H

HOSTING

*Things to Consider if You Want
to Put on Your Own Events*

A fter you have spoken at a few events for other promoters you may want to consider putting on your own event. After all, it looks so easy, doesn't it?

Well not so fast cowboy. Putting on live events of any type is an entirely different business and has to be treated as such. It is one thing to come into another person's event and do a presentation and quite another thing to be the one doing all the legwork behind the scenes to pull off an event.

The first question you need to answer is what kind of event do you want to put on? Will it be a small informal hands-on workshop with 10 of your best clients, a multi-day event with you as the sole trainer for the entire event, or a multi-speaker event with significant back-of-the-room sales?

All three can be great models and there is certainly no right or wrong answer to the question. Each approach has its own pros and cons and you will need to decide which model you want to start with.

Regardless of the model you might choose the first thing you need to evaluate, if you are thinking about doing a live event, is your list. Why your list you might ask? Because your list is where the majority of your event attendees will come from. It will be the people who already know, like and trust you that will be the bulk of your audience.

You are Kidding Yourself if You Think You Can Fill an Event with People Who Aren't Already Really Sold on You

---

You are kidding yourself if you think you can fill an event with people who aren't already really sold on you. If you are going to do a multi-speaker event and think you can fill your room from the lists of your speakers think again. It just is not going to happen.

So you have got to decide if your list is right for an event. Is your list big enough and will they be interested in attending a live event? A lot of first-time event promoters have delusions of grandeur, thinking that they can get half of their list to attend a live event. Most event promoters are doing well to get 1% to 5% of their list members to come to a live event. And this has gotten even tougher over the last few years with the economy. It is getting harder and harder to put butts into seats.

So the key question you need to answer first is "Is your list large enough to support a live event?"

If you decide it is a "go" then we recommend a minimum of 16 weeks lead time to successfully plan and pull off your event. If you already have a system and an experienced team in place you can utilize then you can execute an event with a 12 week schedule.

Expect to wear many different hats when you decide to host your own event. Big money can be made and big money can be lost on a live event and your ability to strike a balance between what you opt to do yourself and what you delegate or outsource to others to do for you will have a massive impact on your overall success.

Entire courses have been written on putting on live events and there is enough information on the subject to fill multiple books. In this chapter we want to give you a taste of some of the issues you may deal with in hosting your own event.

Following is the list of those things you should be doing 16 weeks or more in advance of your event. This is pulled from the SMART™ Seminar Marketing System (SeminarMarketing.com).

Planning
- Conduct strategic planning meeting: determine event objectives and goals, select dates and location (check for industry or local conflicts and inappropriate dates)
- Develop event program; schedule, speakers, content
- Develop preliminary budget

Hotel – Meeting Facility
- Research meeting facilities; send out request for proposal
- Perform on-site review of meeting facility
- Negotiate hotel contract
- Set up master account for meeting charges

Speakers
- Invite Speakers to speak
- Secure Speakers' contract
- Send Speakers information about your event: goals, objectives, audience demographics

- Secure Speaker requirements (audio, visual, etc.)
- Verify and approve Speakers' presentation, product package and pricing
- Verify and approve Speakers' close
- Schedule Speakers' teleseminar call and email to their database to promote event
- Secure any bonuses and/or door prizes Speaker can contribute to event

Event Team
- Select event team and helpers
- Secure helpers
- Select and secure subconsultants (audio/video, bookstore, etc.)
- Make travel arrangements for event

Promoting
- Identify and contact JV partners and/or alliances to assist in promoting
- Identify and contact affiliates to assist in promoting
- Develop on-line and off-line strategy to promote event
- Design website
- Write sales letter (This could take 8-10 weeks—start early)
- Set up shopping cart
- Write autoresponders
- Write broadcast emails
- Create event brochure if promoting through off-line strategies

Wow, seems like a lot, doesn't it? And you may be saying to yourself I don't even know what he is talking about with some of the things on this checklist.

That is why it is critical you educate yourself on all the aspects of hosting your own events. If you decide you are the one who is going to wear the hat in a particular area you better be sure you know what you are getting into.

Dealing with hotels is an art form in itself. A great negotiator like Adryenn can have multiple hotels throwing themselves at her and offering her everything under the sun because she is a pro and understands how it all works.

But, if you don't know how it all works you can really get hosed by the hotels. I had a colleague who did not like the way the wall in a meeting room behind his stage looked. So he ordered a black curtain backdrop behind the stage that dramatically improved the appearance of his room.

But boy, was he shocked at the end of his event when he got the bill and found out that black curtain cost him $6000! Talk about sticker shock.

If the old phrase "You don't know what you don't know" applies to you from an event hosting standpoint you have got to educate yourself first to "Know what you don't know" and our hope is that this chapter will help get you down the road to that understanding.

There is no doubt that hosting your own events can be wildly profitable. It establishes you even more as the expert in your niche, can help you sell more coaching and consulting services and can provide positive cash flow and quick revenue generation.

I have seen multi-speaker events pull in over a million dollars in just a few days. But I have also had event promoters crying on my shoulder because they lost thousands of dollars by not understanding how to negotiate with the hotel.

You have got to know how to do it the right way. So be smart and learn the ropes. As you are speaking at other people's events be sure to study how they are doing what they are doing.

Then, when you are ready to host your own event you can dramatically increase your chances for success.

Chapter I

IMPRESSIONS

Your presentation starts when you walk into the building.

Even if you have spent a lot of time getting ready for a presentation, are confident about its delivery and excited for the audience you are going to present to, it is still possible to big-time blow it, even before you get on stage.

While attending a conference I saw a speaker screaming at a member of the hotel staff in the lobby while the audience was walking into the ballroom. The speaker did not do well.

Another time while sitting in an audience I heard a speaker being rude to someone offstage. He failed to realize his microphone was on and the whole audience heard his tirade before he stepped on the stage. When the emcee asked the audience to give the speaker a warm welcome with applause—no one clapped. We never want you to be the subject of one of these stories.

Your Speech Starts When You Walk
Through the Front Door of the Venue

Recognize that your speech starts when you walk through the front door of the venue. Everyone has their eyes on you - the speaker and everyone's ears are listening to everything you're saying. Present yourself as well off the platform as you do on. This goes for before your speech as well as after. Consider yourself "on" from the moment you get there until your car pulls away from the curb after the event.

Sometimes you are stressed or nervous or running behind- it does not matter. You want to be the best YOU off the platform every time. Follow these tips to ensure your success off the platform as well as on.

Get Your Questions Answered Ahead of Time

Take the time to find out all the details in advance of the event. Where do you park, what room are you meeting in, how many handouts should you bring or will they duplicate them for you? Also, of course, find out how much time you have. You do not want any surprises once you get there. Set yourself up for success in advance of leaving for your speech.

Always Arrive Early

Give yourself plenty of time to get to the venue early. This way you will be relaxed, not rushed, and in a good mood. Then you can give yourself plenty of time to park, locate the meeting room, find the meeting planner and get yourself settled.

Connect With Your Contact

As soon as you arrive connect with whoever needs to know you are there. Ask them if they need anything from you and go over the agenda with them to make sure you are both on the same page. Your contact cannot relax until you are there. The sooner you get there and connect with them the more at ease they will be and that impacts how they work with you.

Assess Your Surroundings

Next, you want to take time to survey the room and make sure people seated in any spot can see you and their view is not blocked. When possible, do not hesitate to rearrange the furniture if necessary. It is key that your meeting room is set up well to support a successful speech or event. Obviously, if you are speaking at a promoter's event the room setup is their choice typically. You can suggest but not dictate the room setup.

Also assess the noise from outside the room. Does a window need to be shut? Does someone need to ask another meeting room to turn down some music? The point of all this is to eliminate all distracting noise. Be quick to close doors and windows if that improves your situation.

Be sure also to ask yourself how is the lighting? Is there enough? Will you or any audience member have glare from a lamp in their eyes? If so, make the necessary adjustments.

If you are using a projector and a screen and slides first make sure it is off to the side so it does not take up the power position for speaking, which is the center of the room. Then pull up your slides and go through them. Be aware that when your slides are on someone else's computer the words or graphics can sometimes get askew and by going through them ahead of time you can fix any that need adjusting.

Find Your Introducer

Go over your introduction with whoever is introducing you. Have them practice, point out the words people usually mispronounce. By the way, always bring two copies of your introduction to the event. It is amazing how often introducers can loose introductions between the hallway and the podium.

As a side note, if there is someone in the audience who knows you, they are the best person to introduce you. They will do a much better job than someone who has never met you and does not know how fabulous you are.

Meet Your Audience

When the first guest arrives or the first person walks into the room, you always want to be set up for your presentation and 100% ready to go. You have checked your microphone, your product table is all set and, if you are using handouts, you know where they are and how they will be distributed. Get everything related to your presentation out of the way so you can put all your attention on greeting and getting to know the audience members before your speech and put all your attention on them.

Some speakers do not do this—big mistake. By taking time to get to know your audience they are going to be much more open to your message and much more engaged in your talk.

Mingle and Mix Before Your Presentation

Introduce yourself to as many members of the audience as time allows. In a small audience, if possible, meet everyone before the presentation begins.

Ask people questions about themselves, what they do and what do they want to get out of the presentation. Get to know your audience as much as possible. The more you have connected with the audience the more they will support you during your presentation.

Smile and Be Approachable

Sometimes when we are a little nervous before a talk we look really serious. Even though you may be nervous before a presentation, you want to appear calm and prepared. Remind yourself to smile, be friendly, make eye contact and be approachable.

Have a firm handshake. Be the kind of person that leans in, makes eye contact and extends your hand first with a big smile. Being friendly off the platform will have you be perceived as an even better speaker on the platform.

Don't Get Stuck with the Other Speakers

Sometimes there is a tendency to stay with your peers. Oftentimes at conferences they have a VIP lounge just for the speakers. Other times there are reserved luncheon tables just for the speakers. Do not connect only with the speakers. There are probably no new clients there. Instead, connect with the audience members, have lunch with the audience members and stay long after your speech to connect with the audience members.

Alright, it is time to apply what you have learned. Look on your calendar- when is your next speech? Did you get all your questions answered and get all the details? Good if you did. If not, do it now and follow the tips for success provided until it becomes second nature and you will be everyone's favorite speaker in no time.

Chapter J

JOINT VENTURES

J oint Ventures, or JVs for short, is a well-known term within the Internet marketing industry and is traditionally used in the context of two or more marketers doing cross promotion of each other's products.

So Marketer "A" has a list and he promotes Marketer "B's" product to his list. And then Marketer "B" reciprocates at some later point in time. Then Marketer "C" gets involved in the loop and so on and so forth.

Joint ventures done in this way can be very lucrative. You can build a list quickly by being able to piggyback on another marketer's large email list and also generate significant amounts of revenue during a new product launch if you are able to work with some powerful joint venture partners.

But there is a downside to the use of joint ventures strictly for cross-promotional purposes. The downside is if marketers continually promote new products to each others' lists then eventually all the lists overlap so much that the effectiveness of the promotions over time decreases dramatically.

It can become a type of vicious circle where you are obligated to promote the product of another person to your list because they promoted your product to their list in the past. So, just be aware of both the pros and the cons if you look at joint ventures strictly for cross promotional purposes.

At its root, however, JVs can refer to much more then just the cross promotion of products between two or more marketers. Any type of collaboration between two or more parties for business purposes can be considered a joint venture. And collaboration can mean many different things.

Take Advantage of Opportunities to Borrow Credibility From Other, More Well-Known Speakers

For up-and-coming speakers it is important to take advantage of all the opportunities that present themselves to borrow credibility from other, more well-known speakers. This can really move your speaking career ahead more quickly. When you are first starting out and you speak at an event that features one or more well-known speakers you should certainly leverage that. In your marketing materials and on your website do not be shy about stating that you have shared the stage with Speaker A, Speaker B or whoever it might be.

There are some events where you can even buy a speaking slot on their platform by becoming an event sponsor. And, if you have the ability to get yourself equal billing with big name speakers for an upcoming event by helping the event promoter publicize the event then take advantage of that opportunity. Put your efforts behind their efforts and maybe you can be one of the headliners also.

You can also associate yourself with more well-known people by possibly collaborating with them in other ways. One colleague of ours wanted to establish herself in a new niche and did it by interviewing the leading experts in that particular niche.

She essentially took the "reporter" role and borrowed the credibility of the experts she was interviewing by being the interviewer.

Others have joined together to create a product that both persons then marketed independently. Again, by tying your name with other more well-known personalities you can "borrow" their credibility to help establish yourself within the marketplace.

We will talk elsewhere in this book about the importance of having one or more of your own books. But, if you are just starting out it may make sense initially to do a collaborative book where multiple authors each submit a chapter to a book. This makes you a co-author hopefully with other known and respected people within your area of expertise.

Our own Caterina Rando offers a kick butt collaborative book publishing program that you should check out if you are not yet ready for your own book.

If, in addition to being a public speaker, you also provide products or services to clients of yours who are well-known within the industry then be sure to ask for testimonials from those you have served that you can utilize in your marketing materials. Testimonials are just another way to borrow credibility from others.

Remember, there is nothing wrong with borrowing credibility. Once you have shared the stage with a big-name speaker do not be bashful about using that to your advantage.

Chapter K

KEEPING IT REAL

Authenticity is a word that is bandied about so much that has almost become meaningless. There are some big name public speakers that use the word "authentic" who are some of the most inauthentic people we have ever seen. You see them up on stage and they wow you and then you see them backstage and they are screaming at their staff to close-close-close. There is a total incongruity between the on stage persona and the real person.

So what does being "authentic" mean to you as a public speaker? It means to be yourself 24/7 and to not put on false airs about who you are. Some speakers are told to "Fake it till you make it" and the danger is that when people find out that you are not what you really present yourself as on stage (and they will find out) then you are "busted" and word will quickly spread.

Did you ever meet someone in person and find that the real person did not match up with their online personality whatsoever? How did that make you feel? Cheated? Tricked? Deceived?

Let us tell you a story—one that will definitely open your eyes about the importance of being who you are all the time.

A few years ago I was having lunch with a colleague in the financial services industry who had built up an impressive list of 55,000+ subscribers to his email list. He had communicated with his audience over a several year period, so they really felt like they knew him well. He had built up that know, like and trust factor that is so important.

One month he decided to do a new email campaign and contracted with a well-known Internet marketing guru to do the campaign. So an email was written and sent to his list of 55,000+ and it started happening almost immediately....

Unsubscribe—Unsubscribe—Unsubscribe—Unsubscribe.... And on and on.

When all was said and done a list that had been numbered at 55,000+ was nearly totally decimated and a list of only just over 5,000 people remained. Ouch! That had to be terrifying to our financial services friend.

Why? Because the email communication that was sent out wasn't "real." It was not what this guy's followers had come to expect from him. It was not his brand. It was not his tone. It was not his "look and feel". In other words, it was not the real him.

That is why it is so critically important that if you are outsourcing any aspect of your marketing or social media communications to others that they fully understand who the real you is. They must know your brand inside out and they must communicate it in the same language and tone in which you communicate.

When you first get into public speaking you will definitely want to have a mentor to show you the ropes. You might get some training on teaching styles or closing techniques or any other aspect of public speaking.

You definitely want someone who will be brutally honest with you. They should up front about the challenges of the speaking profession and not hesitate to tell you where you are going to have trouble. They should be able to offer you advice on what the best thing for you to be selling from the platform is (if you are a platform seller) and give you guidance on best how to practice and perfect your craft.

But, even after you have learned their special "tricks of the trade," at your core you have to remember to be who you really are. It is your personality that will win over the audience and it is your story that they will relate to. Do not be afraid to be transparent and to share a painful truth—it will really win your audience over.

In most cases, your complete transparency will enable you to build a far better rapport with your audience. And, if you are selling from the platform, in most cases your sales will probably increase significantly also. Being "real" is that powerful.

And that "realness" should also spread to your online social media world. It is a big mistake and a big turnoff for your potential audience if your online communications are nothing but pure business and what they can buy from you. People want to know you are human— they want to see the real you. It is okay to share your flaws and imperfections.

There should always be 2 to 5 things that you are radically transparent about. Subjects that are so personal to you that you can talk about them with anybody at any time.

In Adryenn's case they are:

- Gluten free cooking
- Child with ADD
- Home schooling
- Shoe collection
- Foodie

What are yours?

The best compliment you can get is when someone comes up to you for the first time in person and tells you that you are exactly like your online personality. You know you are doing it right when someone tells you they feel like they already know you.

Now being the "real" you does not mean there are times when you would not, for example, filter your language appropriately based on the audience to whom you are speaking. A presentation with a few "F bombs" dropped in might work great if you are speaking to the local union guys. But you would not even think of using that same language with a group of high school students. Use your common sense obviously.

Many speakers think that the way to win a crowd over is to razzle and dazzle them with all the fancy toys they have. They show the picture of their giant mansion and the private airplane and all of their other cool gadgets and such and think people will be so impressed that they will naturally win them over. And it will probably win some people over. That is human nature.

***The True Sharing of Your Heart Really Builds
Audience Rapport and Wins People Over***

But it is the true sharing of your heart that really builds audience rapport and wins people over. And being consistent both on stage and off with who you really are that keeps them as a member of your "fan club" over the long term.

Believe us, the "frauds" eventually get uncovered. They may have a short run of success in the marketplace, but once the inconsistency of the stage persona with the real person is exposed then their following seems to dwindle precipitously.

You have to be able to deliver what you promise when you are a platform speaker. Part of that promise is certainly the consistent delivery of the products and/or services that you might sell from the platform. But another part of it is also that you deliver the real you each and every time you step on that stage.

Promoters do talk and once the word spreads around the circuit about you being a person who is not what they were originally purported to be then your speaking opportunities will begin to decrease also.

With all apologies aside, Coca-Cola™ is not the real thing. You being yourself at all times is the real thing.

Chapter L

LEVERAGE

f you are a speaker and your business is up and going at all, you can quickly find yourself wearing any or all of these hats (and more):

- Public Speaker
- Marketer of Your Speaking Services
- Information Product Developer
- Shipping Manager
- Customer Service Manager
- Order Taker
- Travel Planner
- Website Designer

So you have to ask yourself which of these hats you should be wearing. Where should you be applying your time and efforts to maximize your speaking business? In other words, how can you achieve leverage?

When you are starting out there are certainly some things that you will need to do for yourself. You should have an understanding of all the processes involved with your speaking business.

But, if your business is growing, you will quickly find out that too much of your time is being spent on the mundane tasks—preparing event materials, running down to the post office or UPS, packaging things together, making travel arrangements, etc.

This means you are probably not spending your time where you get the biggest bang for your buck—marketing your products and services and doing the actual speaking.

Business Amplifiers are the Keys to Building a Real Speaking Business

---

So when is the right time to outsource any of the non-key tasks? Ultimately, you will have to decide when that time is for yourself. But what do you value your time at? $50 per hour, $100 per hour, $200 per hour, more? Then how long does it make sense for you to be spending your time doing $10 or $20 per hour tasks?

If you are spending an hour per day running products to the post office that is one hour you are not investing in your real bread and butter. And what is your opportunity cost? The time you are spending on a $10 an hour task is time that is lost forever.

When you are spending time working in your business rather than working on your business then opportunities will slip by without you even noticing them.

There is a time when outsourcing certain tasks makes perfect sense—both from a time management standpoint and from a financial standpoint.

So, when is that time right for you?

As you work to grow your speaking business, if you think you can do it all yourself, you are only kidding yourself. There are probably many things you are doing that you should really outsource if you want to grow your business even faster.

Virtual assistants are available to handle many of your routine tasks. This can allow you to focus your efforts on the more valuable activities of speaking, sales and marketing and product creation. Services like eLance, Rent-a-Coder, and ScriptLance can be utilized to help with product creation. Ghostwriters can write content for you.

But outsourcing is not the only way you can get leverage for building your speaking business. It is not the only business "amplifier" available to you. At some point in time, it may make sense to hire an actual employee.

Also, software tools can be considered business "amplifiers." A software tool that allows you to automate a process that saves you time on a regular basis is also a business amplifier and this further allows you to leverage your time.

You will definitely want to have in place an excellent email autoresponder follow up system that can communicate with your prospects automatically. You simply pre-write and load into the system your messages and much of your follow-up work is handled automatically for you.

There are many systems available—Constant Contact, aWeber, Get Response, Infusionsoft and even Bret Ridgway's own Red Oak Cart (see http://RedOakCart.com).

An email autoresponder system becomes especially valuable once you have built up a large following. There are times when you will want to communicate with your followers (what marketing legend Dan Kennedy calls your "herd") and autoresponders are the way to go.

Another consideration regarding leverage is making sure that as you grow your organization you have in place well developed and documented processes and procedures. Your staff, whether they are actual employees or virtual assistants, should be well-trained and do things in a consistent manner.

Spending time constantly redoing things or being so unorganized you waste time trying to find the things you need are both productivity killers. These are not the ways you want to leverage your efforts.

By its very nature public speaking is a leveraged activity. When you are speaking to many people rather than just to one you are employing leverage. But also think about how you can use tools like pre-recorded webinars to deliver presentations for you automatically that do not require you to travel somewhere in order to deliver your message.

Once you have honed your live presentations to where the response to your call to action from your presentation—whether it is the sale of a product or service or simply an invitation to join your email list— has been maximized then definitely look at pre-recorded webinars as a valuable way to further leverage your time.

Remember, only you can decide what tasks and when things should be outsourced in order to leverage your time more effectively. There may be some things you love doing so much that you want to continue doing them even though you know they are probably not worthy of your time. But it is YOUR speaking business and you are the one calling the shots.

We know a guy who is a speaker who also sells products online who loves running down to the post office every afternoon. It is his mental break from the rigors of his day. And that is okay—he is his own boss.

Another big time speaker we know loves to do his own graphics and his own websites. And has so for years. He continues to do them because they are tasks he finds enjoyable—even if they are not necessarily the most efficient use of his time.

There is a term bantered about frequently in the information marketing world called "repurposing." It means taking content you have already creating and using it again in other ways.

For example, when you are a speaker you might have a stage presentation recorded. You can have that presentation transcribed and turned into articles you can use to help market your speaking services. Or maybe you can burn your presentation to a DVD and sell it as a separate product. So people can experience your presentation without you having to do it live. Both are examples of repurposing.

Repurposing is just another example of leverage. Rather than starting with a blank slate every time look at the content you have already created. Figure out how you can reuse it in your marketing or as a product that you sell.

So, in summary, keep in mind that leverage can come from many different sources:

- Outsourcing
- Employees
- Software
- Automated Webinars
- Repurposing of Content
- Standardized Processes and Procedures

If you are serious about building your speaking business then you will want to employ many different business amplifiers. Leverage is a critical component of building any business, including your speaking business.

Chapter M

METRICS

W hen running any business there's an old expression—"You've got to know your numbers." Yet it is surprising that most business owners have little knowledge of what their key numbers, or metrics are.

Baseball players have their Batting Average, investors have their ROI, Internet marketers have their Click Thru Rate and so on. Each industry has its own set of metrics and the speaking profession is no different.

So what are the metrics you need to look at as a speaker? At any event you speak at there are several key numbers you must know and track from event to event to see how you are performing. These include:

- Number of Attendees
- Number of Buying Units
- Closing Percentage

Number of Attendees

This one is fairly obvious. How many people are in the room at the beginning of your presentation and how many are in the room at the conclusion? Don't try to count them yourself. Enlist the aid of your assistant if you brought one to the event or get the help of someone else you know and trust to do this for you. It is important to get both the starting and ending counts. Don't ever take the promoter's word on the number of people in the room—double check it.

With a large crowd you may find it difficult to get an accurate count. If you get to the event early do a count of how many people the room is set up for. This figure may help you get a more accurate estimate if you are forced to go that route.

Number of Buying Units

While similar to the number of attendees, it is not the same thing. While a husband and wife attending together would be counted as two attendees in your numbers they would be counted only as one buying unit. Why? Because both are not likely to buy the same product at an event.

I was attending an event a few years ago that was aimed at the home school market. Parents were encouraged to bring their entire families to the event and there were nearly one hundred people in attendance. However, when you got down to figuring the number of fathers, mothers, sons and daughters in the audience you soon realized the one hundred people actually represented only about twenty buying units.

Determining the actual number of buying units in a room can be very challenging. In addition to family units you may also have business partners or a business owner and his assistant or even his entire team in the audience. All add to the trickiness of determining the actual number of buying units in the crowd.

You also have to factor in things such as the number of others speakers and their assistants who may be sitting in the room. Some may be hanging around after their presentation or coming into the room early to get the lay of the land and size up the crowd prior to their speaking slot. Although other speakers may occasionally buy another speaker's product you typically wouldn't consider them buying units when figuring your metrics.

Similarly, the event staff itself should not be counted among your buying units or number of attendees. They are there to assist the event promoter and could be doing anything from running microphones, manning a camera or audio board, passing out handouts or assisting at the sales table. Many are volunteers and if one of them happens to buy your product or service consider it an unexpected bonus.

If possible, see if the event promoter can provide you with a list of attendees prior to the event. Of course, there will always be additions and deletions to the attendees list when the event is actually held but a study of the attendee list in advance can help you determine the number of actual buying units as closely as possible.

Closing Percentage

Why is the number of buying units so critical? Because it is the number on which our third metric—Closing Percentage—should be based. The closing percentage is the key metric that many event promoters will want to know when they are considering putting you on their stage. Do not ever inflate your numbers. If you lie about how well you have sold at other events you will eventually be found out and your credibility will be forever tarnished. Event promoters do talk and believe me, word will get around.

Once you have determined as best you can the actual number of buying units in the room then figuring your closing percentage is simply a matter of dividing the number of units of your product or service you sold by the number of buying units in the room.

Here's a couple of simple examples just to be sure you understand.

Example 1: 100 buying units in the room
14 units sold
Closing percentage = 14/100 = 14%

Example 2: 500 buying units in the room
75 units sold
Closing percentage = 75/500 = 15%

If you offer more than one product from the platform such as a Beginner Package A and an Advanced Package B consider the sale of either of them as one unit and combine the sales of both to figure your total units sold.

Another factor you need to consider these days is that it is fairly common to also live stream an event over the Internet while it is going on. Do not forget to find out from the event promoter how many people were logged into the live stream during your presentation and the number of sales made to those viewers who were not in actual attendance at the event. Be sure to factor these numbers into your total when assessing your performance at an event.

Testing and Tracking

We spoke earlier in this chapter about the importance of tracking your performance from event to event. Equally important to tracking is the concept of testing. There are a number of variables that the professional speaker tracks to see how they impact his or her personal results.

You will have to determine which variables you want to test to see how your results are impacted. It is critical to test only one variable at a time. Otherwise, how will you know which variable had the impact on your results? And only over multiple tests will you be able to draw any meaningful conclusions.

There are always variables which you may not be able to control that can impact your results so you can just do the best you can with those things you can control.

So what are some of the factors that speakers have been known to track and test? Here are just a few:

- For a man, suit with tie vs. suit without a tie
- For a woman, business suit vs. brightly colored dress
- Title of your presentation
- Your offer
- Inclusion or exclusion of different bonuses
- Temperature of room
- How certain key parts of your presentation are worded
- PowerPoint vs. no PowerPoint
- Product to be delivered at the event vs. shipped later
- Physical vs. digital product
- Speaking time slot
- Speaker you followed or preceded
- Demographics of audience
- Male vs. female buyers of your offer

This is certainly only a partial list and there are many other variables that one could seriously track and test.

But the professional speaker is meticulous about tracking and testing as many things as they can over time to determine which factors provide him or her with the maximum probability for success.

If you are going to be that professional speaker be sure you are one of the few that really knows your metrics and be sure to track and test those things that influence your results. It will mean more money in your pocket and help provide you with the dream speaking career you envisioned for yourself.

If You Don't Know Your Numbers
You Don't Know Anything

Chapter N

NETWORKING
Use Speaking to Build Yours

I always say it is better to be in the front of the room speaking than in the back of the room listening! Why? When you are the speaker, you open the door to making new, great contacts that can lead to new, great business.

When you are the speaker, you are the one who comes home with the most business and the most new contacts. In the front of the room, you meet everyone in the room, even if they do not meet you. You cannot get more exposure than this.

Here are some tips for improving your ability to build your network when you speak in order to attract new opportunities, clients, alliances, contacts and resources for your business and for your clients so that you reach your goals with more ease.

Get Booked to Speak to Build Strategic Alliances

No matter how competent you are, you cannot grow your business if you stay in touch with only clients, past clients and people who have expressed an interest in working with you. Make sure each of your marketing activities includes a way to gather new contact information from people who are interested in what you do, not just those who already have benefited from your value-based marketing activities. Your goal is to build strategic alliances with people for your mutual benefit.

What do I mean by a "strategic alliance"? I am talking about forging a relationship with someone whose list of contacts is comprised of people who compliment your business. These are people you want to meet and do business with.

For example, in my publishing business www.ThriveBooks.com, when working on a book in a particular topic area where I have few contacts I have cultivated strategic partners who have contacts and connections in those areas such as image consulting, etiquette and civility. Ask yourself these key questions to determine who you want to add to your network through speaking:

- Who is more connected than you to the people you want to connect with?
- Where do you need to build strategic alliances?
- What areas do you want to pursue?
- Whom do you need in your network to grow your business?
- Who in your current network is a potential strategic ally?
- What are the major industries and businesses to whom you currently market?
- What new industries and businesses do you want to add to your market mix?

When you answer these questions, you will begin to identify the types of strategic alliances you want to make. After you define your ideal strategic allies, identify groups where they gather. Ask your current clients what groups they belong to, do a Google® search for groups in your local area and check the calendar listings in your local paper.

Get Booked to Speak at the Groups
Where the People You Want to Build
Alliances with are Gathered

Get booked to speak at the groups where the people you want to build alliances with are gathered. Get to know them, discover what other organizations they are members of and find out how long they have been in business. Generally, the longer someone has been in business, the larger their list of contacts.

Come Away with Strategic Alliance Partners

After your talk, mingle and meet people. If you have brought products to sell at the back of the room, stand at the table and greet people. Walk around; work the room. Take risks, put yourself out there, be willing to act like the host or hostess and extend yourself first to new people.

Seek out the potential strategic allies you have identified to meet and introduce yourself. If you have not identified specific people you want to meet, network. Exchange business cards and state you would like to get to know the person better. Your goal is to meet influential people who could become strategic allies for you and build a long-term, mutually beneficial relationship with them.

When I want to meet people, I walk up to them, extend my hand and say, "Hi, I haven't met you yet. I'm Caterina." This assertive introduction is always welcomed because people appreciate being noticed. It is an easy way to start a conversation.

Once you introduce yourself, remember the person's name. Learning names is a simple skill that can be easily developed. To remember names, use the following tips:

- Tell yourself that you are going to remember the names of new people you meet.
- When introducing yourself, relax and focus on the other person's name. Repeat it back to them by saying, "Nice to meet you, _____."
- Make sure you pronounce the name correctly.
- If you are not sure how to spell the name, ask. This will help you remember it.
- Use the name in conversation in the first two minutes.
- When you end your conversation, use the person's name again.
- Ask for a card and connect the face with the name on their card.
- When you have a few moments, scan the room and repeat to yourself the names of everyone you have met.
- On the way home, mentally run through all your new acquaintances and their names.

How do you know if someone is a potential strategic ally? You ask questions about them. To get a conversation going and make it easy to get to know the people you are meeting, use the following list of questions.

- How did you get started in the _____ business or industry?
- What do you enjoy most about the _____ business or industry?
- How does your company stand out in the _____ industry?

- What is the most exciting thing going on in your industry?
- What risk would you take in your career if you knew you could not fail?
- What are the biggest challenges you are facing currently in your career or business?
- What do you see as the coming trends in the _____ industry?
- What is the funniest or strangest incident you have experienced in the _____ business or industry?
- What is the most effective way for you to promote your business, product or service?
- What would help right now to make your job easier?

Follow Up Fast

The day after your speech, take any actions you committed to. Make calls and send out your follow-up notes. In this day of electronic mail, people appreciate a handwritten note. Enclose your business card even if you gave it to the person the day before. In addition, when leaving messages, it has been shown that the shorter a phone message is, the quicker it is returned.

Enter into your database information for people you want to maintain contact with. Note where you met them and a little information about them. Also, put them into any categories that are applicable. Record information that is important to them—spouse's name, professional affiliations, awards won and so on.

Set goals to connect regularly with the people you have identified as strategic allies and commit to building alliances with them to your *mutual benefit*. Once you get to know your strategic partners, suggest ways you can help each others business grow and prosper. Do events together and cross-pollinate each others contact list.

Start today to identify potential strategic partners and how to connect with them. Set a goal to market and deliver at least two speeches each month that put you in front of potential strategic allies. The sooner you start, the more committed you are, the more speeches you give, the more strategic alliances you will build and the more your business will grow and prosper.

Get busy. Find your potential alliance audiences and get yourself booked. You will be thrilled you did, and your business growth will reflect it.

Chapter O

OFFERS
Selling from the Stage

W e talked in an earlier chapter about speaking models and the choice you will have to make as to whether you are going to be primarily a for "Fee" (Keynote speaker) or a for "Free" speaker who makes your living from product sales at the event.

If you have opted for the latter—the product sales model, then that means your income will be directly related to your effectiveness in selling from the platform.

I have seen speakers deliver great content and then freeze up when it came to the sales close portion of their presentation and I have seen speakers deliver poor content and then do great when they got to their close.

Your objective is to obviously be able to do both—deliver great content and then do a great sales job from the platform. Remember, your first responsibility is to your audience and your obligation is to deliver them great content. In a typical presentation at least

80% of your time should be spent on content and only 20% on your close.

That means in a 90 minute presentation roughly the first 75 minutes should be spent teaching and only in the last 15 will you be doing any selling. Of course, you are "selling" yourself throughout the course of your presentation by sharing your expertise in a way that makes them want to learn more from you. The reaction you are looking for is something like "Man, if what he's teaching us here for free is this good his other stuff must really be great!"

The Transition from the Content Portion of Your Presentation to the Sales Portion Should be Seamless

The transition from the content portion of your presentation to the sales portion of your presentation should be seamless. I've heard too many speakers change their tone or pace when they got to their close and not even recognize that they were doing it. And, believe me, the audience hears it too and you can just feel the barriers immediately go up from the crowd when they now feel they are being sold to.

Believe me, the entire dynamics of a presentation change when you are selling at the end of your presentation rather than delivering content only. Some speakers can get on stage all day long and share content but ask them to sell something at the end and it makes them squeamish.

It does take time and practice to make that smooth transition from content to close. But there a lot of other things going on that you will want to pay close attention to. As you watch other speakers selling from the platform take notice of what they are doing. Here are just some of the things you should be watching carefully:

- How do they handle their transition?
- What do they include in their offer?
- Is their offer simple or complex?
- Are they offering multiple options?
- Do they pass out order forms or direct people to the sales table?
- Do they utilize a single or two-step closing process?
- Are they selling digital or physical goods or some combination of both?
- Are they delivering product right at the event?
- What is the price point of their offer?
- Are they offering payment plans?

Let's dive into each of these questions in a bit more detail. We have already talked about the transition, so let's move on to the offer related questions.

First, you will need to decide what it is you are going to sell from the platform. Will you sell one-on-one coaching with you, group coaching, a physical product, a webinar or teleseminar series, or some combination of these things? There is no wrong or right answer. I've seen all variations sold very effectively from the platform.

You certainly want to create a compelling offer. But, from my experience, it is much more about the quality of the content you deliver and the rapport you establish with your audience that leads to back of the room success then anything else. You can pretty much bundle anything together and have a "winner" if you are a great speaker and can effectively manage your close.

Some speakers adhere to the "more is better" philosophy and stack on item after item into their offer. They present a total value of some gigantic amount and then they do price drop after price drop until they reach their actual selling price. So it seems to them like it should be a no-brainer to take their offer because they are giving you so much for relatively so little.

I have seen this approach work great and I have seen it fail miserably. If the value to price proposition seems to be out of whack then it may seem unbelievable to the audience and you can come across as the stereotypical used car salesman.

And if you are speaking at a multi-speaker event and if some of the speakers that preceded you during the event used a similar closing technique as you, then your "But wait, there's more" may come across as copycatish and as a bit of a joke.

One thing most speakers don't do well that could significantly improve their performance is find out what all the other speakers sharing that stage will be speaking about and what they will be offering. Then, try to be different. We're not saying don't be authentic and continue to deliver great content. We are saying that if they sell a price "x" then you may want to sell at price "y". If they are going to offer A, B, and C in their offer you may want to offer X, Y and Z. If they are offering only a digital product then you offer a physical product. Be different.

I have been at events where the promoter had three different people speak about copywriting. So, if you were the third speaker in that group in the event what would you do to differentiate yourself? If you are the third one offering a $2,000 package of copywriting training and resources then the attractiveness of your offer will be much lower because the audience has already "been there, done that" in their mind.

Only over time, by testing different offers, will you get a true feel of what works best for you. Do you do better at a $497 price point, a $997 price point or a $1997 price point? Or more? Do you sell better if you offer a physical product they can take right with them from the event or with a digital only delivery through a membership site? Do you do better if you offer payment plans or not?

Do you sell better offering a single package or with good, better and best options? Believe me, there is a continuing hot debate on this question. Some say "A confused mind never buys" and others say the more options you give them the better are your chances of getting them to buy something. Only through testing will you find out what works best for you.

Do you sell better if you pass out order forms to the audience near the end of your presentation or if you just direct them to the sales table to get an order form? If you are selling a high ticket coaching program do you do better with a single or a two-step sales process?

You can see all the variables involved in the sales process. You need to continually test and tweak your closes to figure out which combination of options pulls the best for you over time. Keep honing and improving and watch your sales success grow!

Chapter P

PROMOTERS

E vent promoters are an interesting breed. If you have been around the block more than once you have probably learned that they tend to be overly optimistic about the number of people who will be in attendance at their event.

This is especially true if they are a first-time promoter. They speak in terms of "wishes" rather then realities. We are not implying in any way that we think they are being intentionally misleading—it is more that they are simply overly optimistic about the size of the crowd they will actually be able to get into the room.

When the economy tanked back in 2008 even event promoters who had a fantastic track record for years in terms of attendance saw a dramatic decrease in the size of their audience.

As a speaker it is of paramount importance that you find out as far as possible in advance of an event how many people will be in the room. We talked in Chapter M about Metrics—those numbers that you need to track from event to event to monitor your own performance.

These same metrics—number of attendees, number of actual buying units, and closing percentages are all numbers that a professional promoter should be able to provide you from their previous events. They should be able to show you a spreadsheet from their earlier events that break down the sales figures by speaker (anonymously of course).

You know you are dealing with a professional promoter when they can provide this data for you easily. If they are unable to, then you are either dealing with a first time promoter who does not have any historical data, or you are dealing with a promoter who is being less then forthcoming with you and you need to enter into that relationship with your eyes wide open.

An event promoter should always be willing to share with you who else is going to be on their platform. Are all the speaking slots "selling" slots or are they interspersing content only sessions throughout the event?

They should be able to tell you what topic each of the other speakers is talking about, how long of a speaking slot you and each of the other speakers has, and at what price point the others speakers' offers are going to be.

If they have held previous events any information they can provide you about the demographics of their audience and what has worked well from the standpoint of price point and type of products/services offered to their crowd will be beneficial to you.

Remember, promoters put on events to make money. In an ideal world most hope to make enough money from advance ticket sales to cover their out-of-pocket costs for putting on the event. That means that their split of their back-of-the-room sales is where they really make their profits and anything they can do to help you succeed on their platform is only of benefit to them. They are in it for the money.

Speaking of money, you will want to find out from the promoter who handles the money at their event. Are they handling all the order processing and paying you after the fact? Are you collecting your own sales and then paying the promoter after the fact? Or, are they bringing in a third party service like Speaker Fulfillment Services to handle all the money and pay both the promoter and you?

As a speaker, if they give you the option of processing your own sales at the event then you will want to take advantage of this. It is always better for you to control the money if you can. Obviously, you are on your honor to pay the promoter his or her portion in a prompt manner.

If the promoter or a third party is processing the back-of-the-room event sales you need to find out when you can expect to be paid. Some promoters are notorious for being slow (or no) payers and you will want to avoid their platforms if at all possible. You should be able to find out who has spoken at their events in the past and find out what the payment experience of previous speakers has been.

If the promoter or a third party is processing do not expect to be paid prior to thirty days after the event has ended. Why? Because the promoter needs to be sure any refund windows have passed. They do not want to pay you for a sale that is later refunded and have to come back to you to reclaim money you have already been paid.

Remember, the typical split of your sales at an event will be 50/50 of your sales price. If the promoter is collecting the money they will typically cover any credit card fees out of their portion and you will absorb any of the hard costs of delivery of whatever it is you sold on their platform.

But some promoters offer different deals and it is incumbent on you to fully understand what you are getting into. Some promoters take 70% of the sales and you get only 30%. Other promoters will penalize you if you go over your time during your speaking slot. For example, every 5 minutes you go over your allotted time costs you an additional 5% of your back of the room sales.

Carefully Read and Re-Read
Any Speaker Contract Before Signing It

Obviously, these are details that should be covered fully in your speaker contract which you will want to carefully read and re-read before you ever sign it. In some cases you may be able to amend the terms and in other cases it will be a take it or leave it agreement. Just know fully what you are getting into in advance of any speaking engagement you accept.

Another key detail to work out with a promoter is the speaking slot to which you will be assigned. There are certain speakers who come into an event who are fantastic closers and, if they appear on the platform just before you, they will suck all the money out of the room and your closing percentages will drop dramatically.

If you have any sway with the promoter at all you will want to make sure you are speaking before this person rather than after. As far as the best speaking slots at an event, most speakers we know prefer to be either the second speaker in the morning or the second in the afternoon. They want to be sure there is an adequate length break scheduled after the conclusion of their presentation so they have time to answer questions and help at the sales table before another speaker gets on stage and command their attention.

But there are other speakers who love to speak first thing in the morning and make it work very well. There are others who want to be the event closer and do a great job at it.

When you are first beginning your speaking career you will probably have very little input into the speaking slot you are assigned. Be fully prepared to "pay your dues" and accept some early morning slots or other typically non-desired times. It is part of the game.

Vendors are a variable that can also influence your sales at an event. If the promoter is having exhibitors then usually that will have an impact on the back-of-the-room sales, as those vendors may also be pulling money from the crowd. Again, as a speaker this is something you are probably not going to have any control over, but do need to recognize the impact it can have on your sales numbers.

By and large promoters are there to help you. They want to see you succeed because your success puts money into their pocket. Just be sure you understand where they are coming from and that it is their rules you will need to play by if you want to play in their sandbox.

Chapter Q

QUALITY VS. QUANTITY
Creating Your Criteria

W hen you first enter the world of speaking it is highly recommended that you take advantage of almost any speaking opportunity that presents itself. The more practice you can get in front of a live audience, the more comfortable you will feel with your materials and the smoother your presentations will be.

You will learn how to build rapport with your audience better and how to read your audience far more effectively. That ability to read your audience will enable you to adjust your presentations when needed in order to better connect.

But there will come a point in time that you have mastered your presentation (or presentations) and are doing such an outstanding job that you have become a highly in-demand speaker. Opportunity after opportunity seems to be coming your way and, where before you felt like you were begging for every speaking gig, now they are pouring in like the proverbial fire hose.

But there will probably also come a time when you notice that you are not getting the results you want. Maybe your closing percentage is starting to dwindle a little or maybe the applause is not quite as loud when you have finished your presentation. Chances are you have reached the point where you just are not being picky enough about where you speak.

Do You Want More Clients
Or Do You Want Better Clients?

It is the same thing as with clients—do you want more clients or do you want better clients? In the speaking world it will be do you want more speaking gigs or do you want better speaking gigs?

Again, initially we feel like you need to get on as many appropriate platforms as possible so you can hone your craft and really polish up your presentations. But, eventually you will need to be more selective if you are going to get the results you want to achieve.

It comes down to establishing what your speaking criteria are. It really is the Pareto Principle, or the old 80/20 rule as most of us know it. If 80% of your speaking results are coming from 20% of what you are doing then simply do more of that 20% and cut out the 80%.

First, though, you need to determine what your end game is. What longer-term objective is your speaking supposed to lead you closer to? If, for example, your goal is to do television then anything you are doing that does not lead you closer to your end objective should be eliminated.

So, whenever a speaking opportunity presents itself you need to decide if speaking to that particular audience helps you move closer to your goal. It is your job to determine who is your ideal audience. Then, simply make connections with those promoters who are serving the audience that you want to reach.

We have all heard the expression "guilty by association." As a speaker, if you chose to speak on platforms of promoters who have bad reputations or treat their staff badly then you will be guilty by association and your own reputation can suffer as a result of those people you hang around with.

We recommend you follow a "No Assholes" policy in terms of both the promoters you chose to work with and the clients you chose to work with. Adryenn once turned down an opportunity to speak to a crowd of 2500 people (where she could have made significant revenue) because she did not want to have her name associated with that particular promoter in any way.

It is obvious you want to speak with the right audience for you. We have seen far too many promoters bring in someone to their event because they were a "name" and then see that speaker go down in flames because they were not the right fit for that audience.

But what other criteria besides being the right "fit" should you look at when determining on what platforms you want to speak? Should you go speak to a crowd of 5 people? Well, if it is the right 5 people then we say yes.

Even things like your willingness to travel will have to be factored into your criteria. Do you only want to speak at local events that are a quick drive from your home? Or, are you willing to be the proverbial "road warrior" and jump on a plane and travel anywhere to present?

Keep in mind that if you are a platform seller rather than a keynote speaker then you are probably going to be responsible for all of your own travel and lodging expenses. That means if you strike out on the sales front then you actually lost money by speaking at an event.

That is not to say that the additional experience you gained and the connections you may have made will not have some separate long-term benefit. But, if you are speaking just for the paycheck, then that formula does not work very well at all.

Be very, very clear to yourself as to what you are willing to do. Know your long-term objective and always ask yourself "Is this speaking engagement going to move me closer to my long-term objective?" If it is great—go for it. If it is not, then you need to give serious thought as to whether you should pass on that opportunity. We understand that sometimes you may need to accept opportunities that are less then ideal but as much as possible you need to stick to your long-range plan.

One criteria we have yet to mention is "Can people afford what it is you will be selling?" Our recommendation is you avoid events where the crowd would be spending their last dollar to buy whatever it is you are offering. Why? Because these are the same people who will come to you in five months, not having even removed the shrink-wrap from the product, and ask you for a refund because they have to pay their rent.

You want to speak and sell where people can afford what it is you are offering. If you find out after you are already at an event that it is an "on their last dime" crowd you may want to adjust what it is you offer or maybe not even make an offer at all. In many cases you may find that those that can afford you will seek you out and an event can be profitable even though you were not selling directly from the stage.

Is *more* better from a speaking perspective? Not necessarily. That is why it is your responsibility as a speaker to determine who the right people are for you. Will you always find a crowd that is 100% the right fit for you? No. But, if you have a clear picture of what your end objective is and who the ideal audience is for you then you will dramatically increase your chances for success at any given event.

Speaking is a wonderful profession. But speaking to the right people makes all the difference in the world in how you will feel about what you are doing and how well you succeed at it. Know who your audience should be.

Chapter R

RESPONSIBILITY

R esponsibility—now there is one wide encompassing term. So, what do we mean when we talk about responsibility as a speaker? Responsibility comes into play in several areas when you are a speaker. You have responsibility to:

- Your audience
- Your customers
- Your event promoter
- Your family
- Yourself

So, let us take a look at each of these areas in some depth.

Your Audience

Every time you go on stage you should deliver the absolute best presentation you can. You owe it to your audience, regardless of the size, to give it your very best every time out.

If you are a speaker for very long you will hear about this term called promoter's numbers. What that literally means is the number of attendees that the promoter says will be at their event. Typically, they estimate way too high and you find out that the size of the crowd is smaller then advertised.

Even if you are expecting 100 people and there are only 10 in the room you owe those 10 your very best. Size does not matter in regards to the quality of the effort you will put forth on the stage.

Your Customers

If you are selling your products and/or services at an event then you hope some in the audience will take advantage of your offer. The people that do take you up on your offer now are your customers and you have certain responsibilities to them.

Your first responsibility is be in touch with them quickly after the event (or even during the event) to let them know how much you appreciate them becoming your customer. This will really solidify your relationship with them and hopefully lead to a long-term, mutually beneficial relationship.

Your second responsibility is to deliver to your customers everything you promised they would receive when they purchased from you at the event. It does not matter what they purchased—products, services, webinars, coaching, whatever. You must deliver on your promises.

The speaker who does not deliver on the back end quickly establishes a negative reputation for themselves and word will spread. You will NOT be invited back to stages when you become known as a person who does not deliver what you promised.

A word of warning here—you should never sell a product from the platform that is not completed and 100% tested. I have seen products sold before where the speaker said "This will be ready in just two weeks." But two eventually became four, then five, then six. Even though it was due to factors beyond their control they had to refund every single sale from the event out of their own pocket.

I have also seen speakers sell a non-tested concept. When fully tested the concept did not work and, again, they had to refund every sale. To the tune of $325,000! Ouch.

Your Event Promoter

We have talked elsewhere about how your speech begins once you walk in the front door of the venue. You do owe it to the event promoter to be on time and to be accessible to the audience. Want to be invited back to more events from this promoter? Deliver an outstanding presentation and be the speaker who is willing to bend over backward to accommodate the promoter's needs.

If you are doing back-of-the-room sales and are the one collecting your own sales then you have the responsibility to pay the event promoter in a timely manner. They have relied on you in good faith to handle the sales and they expect to be paid whatever the pre-agreed upon portion of your sales is within around 30 days.

If you offer any type of payment plan on your offer then you need to make sure you collect the additional funds from your customers and pay the promoter on those later collections also.

You also have the responsibility to the promoter to not "harvest" their list without their permission in advance. What does this term mean? The list in this case is the actual attendees at an event. Promoters tend to frown on tactics to capture the contact information of everyone in the room. The promoter is the one who spent their time and money to put the bodies in the seats and those people are their list, not yours.

Of course, if someone buys your offer at an event, if you are selling from the platform, they become your customer and you have every right to communicate with them. Or, if you have agreement in advance from the promoter that some giveaway you are doing to collect the attendees information is okay with the promoter then go ahead. But, typically, the promoter will not take kindly to you harvesting their attendee list and it is your responsibility to make sure you abide by their wishes.

Your Family

If you are doing a lot of speaking then, chances are, you are spending a lot of time away from home. If you plan to take on professional speaking as your full-time vocation, then the support of your family is critical for both your long-term mental health and your long-term business success.

How can you involve your family in your speaking business? If you are speaking to build awareness of your core business and your spouse or significant other is involved with your business then perhaps you can get them to become a speaker also. That way you can share the promotional duties from a speaking perspective.

If they are not involved in your speaking business then see if you can take them on the road with you from time to time. As a speaker, there can be a lot of lonely hours on the road and if you are able to spend more time with your family the travel can go smoother.

Yourself

Maybe this one should be at the top of the list. Be responsible to yourself. You have a lot of obligations as a speaker and many challenges that will be thrown your way. Without getting into a detailed psychological analysis you have essentially got to remain true to yourself.

Whatever your core values and belief systems are what you really answer to. You answer to yourself. Everything you do in terms of how you deal with your audiences, your customers, your event promoters and your family should be rooted in your core beliefs. Anything less just should not be acceptable to you.

We have seen too many speakers focus only on the money at the expense of everything else. Just being in the game for a quick buck and not truly caring about your customers and others will put you on the fast track to failure. Business and personal relationships can crumble if they are not carefully managed.

The seriousness with which you accept the responsibilities you have as a public speaker will go a long way in determining your success as a speaker. But, more importantly, it will go a long way in determining your success in life.

Speaking is a great whether you are using it as a marketing vehicle or whether you have climbed on board full-time as a professional speaker. Be sure you honor all your responsibilities to achieve greater long-term success.

Be Sure You Honor ALL Your Responsibilities as a Speaker

Chapter 5

STORYTELLING
How to Develop Stories to
Be a More Compelling Speaker

"Speech is power: speech is to persuade, to convert, to compel."
—Ralph Waldo Emerson, American essayist

Tips for Becoming a Great Storyteller

P art of becoming a sought after speaker is your ability to share a great story. It's how you connect with your audience and deliver a memorable, take-action message. We might not think we have any good stories to tell, that's not true. Let me share how you can pull stories out of your own life experiences, quickly and with ease.

Here is what you need to know before you get started:

A good story has four parts

1. The set up and situation—Who, what, when and where. This is where you explain what is going on and paint a visual picture for the audience with your word choices.

2. The question, dilemma or problem—Do not start by saying, "I am going to tell you a story." Just begin by sharing what the story is about and why it is significant.

3. The solution or outcome—What happened? How does the story end? Don't leave your audience hanging. They will keep waiting for you to finish the story and it will distract them from hearing the rest of your talk.

4. The relevancy—Why are you telling this story to your audience? What is the point you are making? Why is it relevant?

These four ideas are the foundation for good storytelling. One important point I want to make: Not all of your stories have to be positive and cast you in the best light. Some of your biggest failures make the best stories. Do not be afraid of disclosure, of being vulnerable on the stage. You make your biggest connection when you show your human side.

- Create visual images with your story. Make sure the audience can see in their mind the place and situation you are describing. Show, don't tell. Think of this as a performance. Use eye contact, vocal inflection, hand and body gestures to emphasize what you are saying.

- Collect examples, ideas, anecdotes, quotations, interesting facts and examples. Review these regularly, you never know when you might be able to use them in your talk.

- NEVER TELL A STORY YOU HAVE HEARD ANYONE ELSE TELL. Why? Because it's likely someone has heard it before. That makes your telling of it cliché and it could cost you credibility.

- Do not hesitate to exaggerate, embellish and mix stories together. You're using the story to underline a major point in your talk. It is fine to take some creative license here.
- Eliminate any facts that do not serve the story. Take out everything that complicates and does not support your point.
- Always be looking for ways to improve your storytelling. If you can, make a video of your speech. Ask a trusted friend or colleague how can you upgrade the language, the delivery and your body movements.
- Find a way to connect with your audience. Tell stories they can relate to. If you are very different from your audience, tell stories from people in your life that they can relate to.
- The delivery is most of the story. Rehearse your stories just as you rehearse the rest of your talk. You want to deliver your stories with confidence and certainty.

Now that we've covered the fundamentals of storytelling, here are some ideas to trigger your own story development.

Story Development Worksheets

On a piece of paper, jot down the answers to the following prompts. Take some time to do this, it doesn't have to be done all at once. Be sure to re-visit this exercise a few times. You'll keep uncovering story ideas that will keep your talks fresh and relevant.

- List all the roles you have had both personal and professional. People like to hear how you got your start.
- List all the jobs and careers you ever had, both paid and unpaid.

- What roles and occupations did your parents and grandparents have? Our family stories are our history. An old family tale is just as powerful as one we experienced ourselves.
- List all your achievements large and small, both personal and professional.
- List some of your life's/business disappointments. Our misses can be more compelling than our wins. Why? People like to hear stories about we handle adversity, it inspires them with their own personal challenges.
- What are the places you have visited or lived? Sometimes geographic commonality can forge a deep connection with the audience.
- List some of your life's greatest moments/memories in business.
- What made you pursue this career/ business?
- When did you know this is what you wanted to do for your work? To your audience, you are living the dream. Telling them how you got there inspires them to pursue their own.
- Identify an early memory in your career/business.
- What are some books that you have read/studied? What about movies? This is where you can draw anecdotes and quotes to liven up your talk.
- What are some of the lessons you have learned in your business? Some lessons are universal, others are not. Business growth is rarely smooth. Your side trips can make a great story.
- What was your most embarrassing moment in your business/ career? Again, don't be afraid to share something personal. This is also a great opportunity to tell a funny story. Humor can relieve tension, it can also put people on your side.
- Whom did you admire when you were young? Whom do you admire today in business, or your industry? We all learn from somebody. Who our heroes are, and why, can be very inspiring.

- What is a dream for your business/career that no one knows about?
- List at least two client success stories. This is your chance to tell people what it's like to work with you. It is a subtle way of preparing your audience for the offer you are about to make.
- List at least two of your secrets for success. Like client success stories, how you succeeded in business draws people to you. That's because they believe if you can do it for yourself, you can do it for them.
- What struggles do you see your clients having over and over? Address this question and you prove your knowledge and credibility to the audience.
- What was a defining moment in your career/business life? A defining moment can be one that drives us down the same path or empowers us to take a new direction. Either way, it can be an inspirational story.

Now it's time to study your responses. Some stories are ho-hum, others will just jump off the page. Mark the stories that have depth and resonance, then expand on them. Fill in the details, make sure you are hitting the four storytelling points I mentioned earlier in the chapter. As you make notes, be sure to engage all five senses. This will help your own memories come alive, which in turn helps you tell a better story.

> ### *Your Good Stories are What Will Make You a Sought After Speaker*

Once you outline your stories, practice your delivery. You need to perfect the timing, pacing and emotions you are trying to convey. Your stories will take on a new life with every telling, and that's the idea. Go with the inspiration when you are up on the stage. Your good stories are what will make you a sought after speaker.

Chapter T

TECHNOLOGY
Friend and Foe

As a speaker, technology can be one of your greatest friends. But it can also be one of your greatest enemies, as we have all seen a speaker go down in flames due to a technical glitch in their presentation. Can it be prevented 100% of the time? Of course not, but there are certain steps you can take to minimize the chances of a technology snafu negatively impacting your presentation.

Technology can encompass many things in the speaking world and in this chapter we are going to talk about different technology-related topics—things that can impact you both on the platform and in the back-of-the-room. Things like:

- PowerPoints
- Microphones
- Clickers
- Mobile Technology

- Presenter Tools
- Back-of-the-Room Technology
- And More

PowerPoints

Your effective use of technology in your presentation can have a dramatic impact of your ability to share your message effectively with your audience. For example, if you tend to ramble as a speaker then the use of PowerPoint or Keynote can help keep you on track with your presentation.

You do not want to put into text in your PowerPoints every word that you are going to say. No one wants to hear you read your PowerPoint. We recommend you use a picture to remind yourself what you wanted to talk about next. Your audience will glance at your picture on the screen and then immediately refocus their attention on you directly.

No More then 4-5 Bulleted Items on a Single Slide

If you are going to incorporate text into your PowerPoint then you should have no more then 4-5 bulleted items on a single slide. A combination of text and video is also fine as long as you keep the text to a minimum. You can also incorporate video into a PowerPoint presentation but you should never, ever, ever try to pull a video directly from the Internet, whether it is a YouTube video or something you are pulling from another site.

You simply cannot trust the reliability of an Internet connection in any meeting room, even if the hotel or promoter tells you they have Wi-Fi in place. While an actual live demo of you performing some task online in real time can be impressive, if the Internet connection fails you then it can really kill the momentum of your presentation.

What you should do instead is embed that video right into your PowerPoint so that you are not reliant upon an Internet connection over which you have no control. As a speaker you should always control those things which you have the ability to control to increase your chances of success.

Cross platform issues can also arise with PowerPoints. If you work on a MAC typically, but the event promoter is using a PC-based system at their event then you can have a problem. Never wait until the last minute to make sure your PowerPoint is going to work okay. You should save any presentation to PDF as a backup plan just in case.

Some promoters will allow you to bring your own computer to hook up at the event. Just make sure you know in advance how all of this will be handled so you do not get hit with any unexpected surprises.

Microphones

A second seemingly innocuous technology that can create unexpected problems for you as a speaker is the microphone. There are four basic types of microphones that might be available to you as a speaker. These are handheld microphones, over-the-ear microphones, lavaliere microphones and podium-mounted microphones.

Most people are familiar with your typical handheld microphone. Using this type of microphone can be a real challenge for many speakers, as they tend to be very expressive with their hands and they forget that if you do not hold the microphone at about chin level consistently not everything they say is being heard by their audience.

An over-the-ear microphone frees up your hands if you are that "expressive" speaker that likes to use their hands. If you normally wear earrings however, you may want to be sure they are not dangly earrings if you are using an over the ear microphone, as they can create unwanted noise or other problems.

A lavaliere microphone, also known as a lapel mic, is a small microphone that is typically clipped onto your clothing to allow hands-free operation. The cord may be hidden by your clothes and either run to a radio frequency transmitter or a pocket-sized digital audio recorder that you keep in your pocket or clip to your belt. With a lavaliere microphone you also want to be sure you are not wearing any jewelry or have clothing that can negatively impact your sound quality.

Just as dangly earrings can create an issue with an over-the-ear microphone, a large dangly necklace can create audio issues with a lavaliere microphone. Also, if you have long hair you should wear it over your ears.

When speaking at some events you may be given a podium with a mounted microphone. While we recommend working the entire "stage" to establish better rapport with your audience sometimes that simply is not possible if you have to speak at the podium and the microphone is fixed. Be sure, if at all possible, to get to the microphone in advance of your presentation so you can determine the optimal distance from the microphone from which you should speak.

Clickers

To control your PowerPoint you should always carry with you your own clicker to any event at which you are going to speak. We have seen many a speaker stumble around with a clicker they are unfamiliar with and it can cause a really herky-jerky presentation. You should be well-practiced with your own clicker and know the sensitivity of the buttons.

If you have an opportunity to get on stage prior to your presentation to test the range of your clicker and where you need to point it for best results you should definitely do so. This is also a good time for you to do a pre-presentation run through of your PowerPoint to make sure they are able to play it without issue.

You should also walk around the stage while you are miked up to test for spots you should avoid walking into during your presentation because that spot is sensitive to sound interference that can create an ear shattering unpleasant experience for your audience.

Mobile Technologies

Technologies now exist that can allow you to capture audience information automatically via their smart phones or other portable devices. We have seen some speakers offer a copy of their PowerPoint presentation to the audience if they text something to a certain number. They are then automatically added to their list and they are able to do follow-up marketing to them. With open rates on text messages hovering around 98% it is a very hot technology right now.

Of course, you will want to check in advance with the event promoter to make sure they are okay with you giving their audience something for free. Many will be fine with it, but others may not allow it because they view it as an attempt to "harvest" their list.

Presenter Tools

Many event promoters these days make available to you "tools" to help you keep on track with your presentation. They have given you an allotted time frame and you should stick to it. So you will have a large monitor, typically called a "confidence monitor," in front of the stage facing you that you can see but the audience cannot.

This monitor will show you your PowerPoint and, in some cases, also show you the next slide in your presentation in addition to the current slide that your audience is seeing. You should never have to turn your back to your audience with the monitor in front of the stage facing you.

This monitor can also usually feature a countdown timer that shows you how much time you have left in your presentation. At lower tech events your countdown timer may be nothing more than someone in the back of the room displaying cards that say 30 minutes—15 minutes—10 minutes—5 minutes—Time's Up. If they are going the low-tech route then be sure you know in advance who will be displaying these signs and where they will be standing so you know where to look.

Back-of-the-Room Technologies

If you are speaking at an event that you will be selling at it is important you understand what back-of-the-room order taking technologies will be utilized. First and foremost, who is responsible for processing your sales—you or the promoter?

If the promoter is processing the sales are they doing it in real time or are they just collecting those order forms and processing them later? And who is responsible for providing those order forms—you or the promoter?

If the promoter will be managing the entire sales process be sure they clearly understand what your offer(s) will be in advance. Always make yourself available to answer questions about your offer after your presentation and, if possible, bring your own assistant or trained staff to assist at the sales table, especially if you are selling a big ticket item.

Whether it is you or the promoter actually processing the sales, if you are just taking orders at the event and the processing will occur later, you should always have a triplicate order form - one copy for you, one for the buyer, and one for the promoter.

Triplicate order forms are available at Bret's website MyEventMaterials.com

If responsibility for the processing of your orders falls to you then you will need to decide if you want to process in real time or not. We always recommend real time processing, if possible, because if there are any issues with someone's credit card you can address it on-site rather than having to follow up later. And, obviously, the quicker you process the quicker you will receive the money.

There are some great technologies such as Square you can use with a smart phone or table or other applications that allow you to process your sales on-site. Take advantage of these.

Technology is great. And also sometimes it is a great pain. Plan ahead and test ahead of time whenever you can to avoid problems such as cross channel mismatches and other issues.

Chapter U

UPSELLS AND UNDER-VALUING
How Much Money are You Leaving on the Table as a Speaker?

I recently attended an event and ran across a speaker I have known for several years as a for "fee" keynote speaker only. Let us call him Ted for the purposes of this story. Ted was excited because he had finally completed his first product he could sell from the platform and he realized he would not have to rely only on his speaking fee to generate income.

It was a nice looking product consisting of a six CD set along with an accompanying workbook. When Ted get on the stage he wowed the audience and his product was really in hot demand at the back of the room sales table. He probably sold 20% of the audience on his program, which he had every right to be happy about.

But then I noticed the event promoter over to the side of the sales table kind of slowly shaking her head. She did not say anything to Ted immediately but I was pretty sure I knew exactly why she was shaking her head because I have seen it many times myself at other events.

Ted had done a fantastic presentation. The audience had really responded well to his content and then to his end of talk offer for his CD and workbook set. So he had a hungry crowd lined up at the back table to invest in his $197 CD and workbook set. So that is what he sold them—his $197 set.

What I am sure the promoter was shaking her head about what that Ted seemed to have no grasp of the concept of an upsell.

How Much Money are You Leaving on the Table as a Speaker?

What Is an Upsell?

An upsell is the offer of an additional product or service at the time someone is placing their order. The most common example that people can relate to is the "Would you like fries with that?" line you get at McDonald's™ when you order a Big Mac™. McDonald's knows that a large percentage of the people will say yes and they will make additional profit from that customer on that transaction.

In the world of selling from the platform it is when you have them at the sales table in the back and they have already pulled out their credit card and are placing an order for your product or service. What additional product or service could you offer them that would be of great value to them?

If you truly have additional products or services that could improve their situation you are, in reality, doing your customers a disservice by not even making them aware of it.

Upsells are very popular in the online world. When you are going through the online checkout process you will frequently see a message pop up to the effect of "since you are buying Product A, today you are eligible to also receive Product B for just "x", a savings of "y" off versus buying the products separately. You then have the option of adding that item to your shopping cart or not.

I have seen upsells online work so well that 95% of the people took the upsell. I have also seen situations where the product offered as an upsell was priced at 5X the price of the original product offered. And it worked very well. What you can upsell is really only limited by your own creativity.

Think about infomercials. The $9.97 gadget you initially ordered typically turns into a $60 sale because of the upsells that they do when you call in to place your order.

So what can you upsell during a live event at the sales table? Remember, they are already in a buying mood, so take advantage of that positive momentum and offer them something additional to purchase.

Possible Upsells for the Platform Speaker

Here is just a partial list of possible upsells for a platform speaker:

- Follow-up Teleseminar Series
- Follow-up Webinar Series
- Group Coaching Calls
- One on One Coaching Calls
- Q & A Calls
- Additional CD/DVD Sets
- Tickets to Your Own Live Event
- Access to a Membership Site

It is sometimes a challenge to determine what you should include in your main offer from stage. What should the core offer be? What items should be bonuses? And what products or service should be part of your upsell? It is one of those things you will only determine the best answer to by testing different variations over time.

Avoid Upsell Hell

Just be sure to avoid what we call "Upsell Hell." Upsell Hell is where you almost beat your customer to death with upsell after upsell after upsell after upsell. Just because they have said yes to your first upsell does not mean you want to keep going until they say no. Again, you should test. But if you are going to keep pushing until you get push back you risk upsetting your customers and destroying the goodwill and relationship you have worked so hard to build.

Training the Back of the Room Crew

Of course, if you are going to offer an upsell at the back of the room sales table at a live event it is critical you provide proper training on how to do that upsell to the sales table staff. If you are bringing your own assistant or staff to help at the sales table that's great—most event promoters will welcome the help.

But if the crew is provided entirely by the event promoter it is important to remember that they will probably be working with multiple speakers over the course of the event and are dealing with multiple offers. And the offers all start to blend together after a while and they can become confused. So you probably should not make your upsell overly complex or they will not do a great job of helping you sell it.

Provide a Written Summary Sheet

You should also have a good written summary sheet of both your basic offer and a separate summary sheet for your upsell. People frequently get confused about what they have bought and if you give them a nice written piece after they have purchased that summarizes what they are receiving you will have happier customers and reduce customer service burdens for yourself.

Remember, people will gladly pay good money for your products and services if they provide real value and provide a solution they are looking for. Do not undervalue the value of what you have to offer people, which is another common mistake many speakers make.

Don't Undervalue What You Have to Offer

I am sure the event promoter in our story was also shaking her head about Ted's $197 price point. Event promoters want people that can sell from the stage and put money into their pockets. The back-of-the-room sales is where most promoters make their money and if you are selling a low ticket item it just does not add up to much for the promoter after the 50/50 split of your sales.

Look at your price point. Like anything you need to test and see what works best but price points of $997, $1997 and $2997 or higher are common at many events. Do not be afraid to test higher price points. Just build the value into what you have and see your sales soar.

So, do not Undervalue and do Upsell.

Upsells are powerful. Use them.

Chapter V

VISIBILITY
Social Media Strategies

I n the past few years social media has exploded on the scene and, as a speaker, you certainly need to be in tune with what is happening and using the appropriate social media platform(s) to help you advance your speaking career.

It is easy to get sucked into the time trap that social media can become, so it is important you be very strategic in how you are going to use social media platforms to help you build your speaking platform.

Just take a look at all the platforms that are making noise in the social media world.

Facebook – Twitter – LinkedIn – Google Plus –
Pinterest – YouTube – Foursquare – Vine –
Instagram – Tumblr - Snapchat

By the time this book goes to press there will probably be another two or three platforms that could be added to this list.

Facebook is, of course, the 800 pound gorilla of this group in most people's eyes. But, all the other platforms, be it Twitter, LinkedIn, Google Plus, Pinterest, YouTube, Foursquare, or any other may play a vital role in helping you establish your presence in your marketplace depending on who you have identified as your target market.

Here are brief descriptions of some of the major social media platforms.

Facebook – An online social utility that connects people and organizations with friends and others who work, study, live, and engage around them. People use Facebook to keep up with friends and family and to share links and to share photos and videos of themselves and their friends. They also search Facebook to learn more about people and organizations.

Twitter – A micro-blogging and social utility service that allows users to send and read messages known as tweets, which are text-based posts of no more than 140 characters. People use Twitter to share and view links, pictures, videos, opinions, news, professional information, personal status and more.

LinkedIn – business-oriented online social utility that allows users to strengthen and extend one's existing network of trusted contacts. People use LinkedIn to stay informed about contacts and their industry of interest.

Google Plus – The second largest social networking site in the world, having surpassed Twitter in January 2013. Google has described Google+ as a "social layer" that enhances many of its online properties, unlike conventional social networks generally accessed through a single website.

Pinterest – Favored by women, this platform allows users to 'pin" images from any web page to boards on their profiles. Common topics of boards are crafts, recipes, home decor.

YouTube – A video sharing website on which users can view, upload, and share videos and comments on other's videos.

Foursquare – Allows your friends to know where you are and for you to know where they are. You can also collect points, prizes and "badges."

We talked about "keeping it real" in another chapter, and it is imperative that you be the "real" you on any social media platform in which you participate. Your goal with social media is to make people want to be around you.

You know how, when you go to a party, there are all types of people? Some people are what we call "Eeyores" and nobody wants to be around them. Others seem to be like the prototypical slicked-back hair new insurance salesman who is trying to sell everyone in the room insurance. No one likes either of those types of people.

But if you are the "butterfly" person—the one that seems to flutter from person to person, making sure everyone has a drink and introducing each party guest to other guests then you become the person that everyone wants to be around. It is not about you—it is about everyone else.

That is how you want to be online—you want to be the person making the introductions and sharing content that others want to share. Quotes are a very popular item to share, especially visual quotes. You need to share things that are seriously shareable. And you need to plan for what might happen if something you share goes viral.

And things can go viral. Adryenn once shared with her Facebook followers the picture of a guy who appeared to have half of his face missing. But, if you looked at the picture long enough he appeared to turn his head and you had a totally different perspective. This photo was shared over 37,000 times and received over 64,000 comments.

Now that is building some serious social media juice! The feedback rankings shot through the roof on that posting and Adryenn's position as an influencer was greatly enhanced as was her EdgeRank.

Bottom line, if you are sharing information via any social media platform make sure it is what your audience wants. Remember that it is all about them. Ask them questions. They want to engage with you. You want to drive what is called your "Social Media Credit Score" upwards.

But how do you determine on which social media platform(s) you should be investing your time? It is primarily a question of where the audience you want to reach is hanging out. If you are a Keynote speaker then your audience would primarily be corporate in nature, so you want to focus the bulk of your time on LinkedIn. If you are a platform speaker (sell products from the stage) then Facebook is where you want to spend the majority of your time.

We are not saying you do not want to be involved with the other platforms. You do. But we all have limited time and you need to concentrate your efforts on the platform where your audience is most likely to find you.

You Need to Concentrate Your Social Media Efforts on the Platform Where Your Audience Is Most Likely to Find You

One of the major overlooked benefits of the social media platforms are their value as a market research tool. If there are certain "movers and shakers" in your industry who are people that you want to know (but more importantly you want them to know you) then you can learn a wealth of information about them via their social media profiles.

For example, let us say there is an event promoter on whose stage you would like to appear but you do not have a relationship with them yet. You might start by volunteering at their live event. We have seen many a speaker get to someone's stage by beginning as a volunteer at their event.

But you also want to begin to follow them and interact with them via their social media profiles. On Facebook you should mark them as a close friend so that you see everything that they post on their timeline. Then you begin to comment on their posts and share their posts via Facebook and Twitter.

They will start to see you more and more in their world because you are giving them "Social Media Love". You are helping them to spread their message by your reposting and other activities and, over time, you will get noticed by them. They will begin to recognize your expertise via the insightful comments you make about their posts and your goal is to have them begin to actively engage with you by then reposting things of yours.

Does all of this happen overnight? Of course not. But by being actively engaging with those people via social media who you want to take notice of you then you should gain their attention over time. And then leverage the relationship you have built into potential speaking opportunities.

We have not talked in this chapter yet about YouTube. As a speaker you should definitely have your own YouTube channel. YouTube is essentially a massive search engine for video, and someone looking to potentially book you as a speaker might well go on YouTube to check you out. So make sure you have high quality videos on your own channel.

Social media should be an important part of your marketing mix. Just be sure you manage your time investment in social media marketing appropriately, as it is just one tool in your marketing arsenal.

Chapter W

WRITING A BOOK

T here is no doubt that one of the quickest ways to establish yourself as an expert is to be an author. Make no mistake about it—being a speaker is great. But when you add in the additional fact that you are also the author of a book on the subject on which you speak it can multiply your creditability tenfold.

Speakers and authors both hold a special position in the eye of the general public. In their minds if you a public speaker and you have written a book then you must be the real deal and someone worthy of notice.

Your book can be a great lead source for you for your higher ticket coaching programs and live events. For just a small amount a person can learn more about you and what you have to offer. Or it can be a great business card for you in many situations.

Yet many speakers can't seem to overcome their writer's block or whatever is holding them back from completing their first book. Yet, writing a book need not be difficult and the benefits you will gain from having that book will make it all worthwhile.

Many people think that the only way you can write a book is to sit down with a blank sheet of paper or blank computer screen and start adding words to the page. This is certainly one way to write a book and many do it in exactly this manner. To keep themselves on task they have daily or weekly writing goals that continue to push them toward the completion of their book.

But starting with a blank sheet of paper is certainly not the only way one can write a book. If you are having trouble getting going on your book here are some alternative ways to write your book.

1. Speak your book. If you are a great talker but not such a great writer just get a decent microphone and recording software and say what you want to write. Of course it will need some editing but speaking your book is a great way to get your thoughts into writing. Just have a transcriptionist take that recording and turn it into a written document. No more blank piece of paper!

   Keep in mind that one hour of audio typically translates into about 35 pages of transcripts. So, if your goal is to have a 150 page book then you are going to need about 4-1/2 to 5 hours of audio to transcribe.

2. Take a video recording from you at some live event and have it transcribed to form the basis for your book.

3. Combine a series of articles you have written previously together, organize it appropriately and you have a book.

4. Combine a bunch of blog posts you have done over the last couple years together to form the basis for your book.

5. Have someone do a series of interviews with you and use the transcription of those interviews to make a book.

6. If necessary, start with a compilation book with other authors where you are contributing one chapter only to the book to get started. See Caterina's ThriveBooks.com.

7. Take an existing home study course or other product you have written previously and pull content from that to write your book. Repurposing is a key phrase you need to understand. You don't have to necessarily reinvent the wheel—you may already have content you can reuse in some form as the basis for your book.

8. Hire a ghostwriter to write your book for you.

However you get it done, get it done. Your book is an important weapon in your marketing arsenal and in helping you build your platform as a speaker.

Your Book is an Important Weapon In Your Marketing Arsenal

It should be a key component of your physical media kit. You will want to send it to event promoters on whose platform you want to speak.

As a key component to helping you build your platform as a speaker it is a given that the quality of your book should be outstanding. But even the best of content will go unnoticed if you do not put together your book in a way that encourages the end reader to read your book from cover to cover. In other words, it is all about product consumption.

So how do you make your book more consumable for the reader? I recently went into a Barnes and Noble and picked up a book in the business section on marketing that sounded kind of interesting based on the title. So I picked it up off the shelf and began to browse through it.

I took a look at the first chapter and began thumbing through it. The first chapter went on for not 10, not 20, but for 35 pages! My thought was "If it's going to be this much work to get through just the first chapter then I don't even want to start reading this book."

People like to consume information in bite-sized chunks. When you overwhelm them with lengthy chapters you make it nearly impossible for the reader to feel that intermittent sense of accomplishment that comes from completing a chapter. So the answer is obvious. Divide your chapters into more reasonable consumable segments—a maximum of 7-10 pages per chapter. Look at this book and you will notice chapters of only 4-5 pages in length on average.

You will also notice that each paragraph is only two to three sentences in most cases. It is all laid out with the thought of bite-sized chunks to help you consume the information more easily. Avoid overwhelmingly long paragraphs that intimidate the reader and stifle consumption.

Utilize pull quotes, boxed case studies, bulleted lists, illustrations, graphs, charts and other things that help break up the page so that everything is not pure text. Bottom line, if you make it easier on the eye you make it easier for the reader to consume.

Also avoid teeny tiny font that is difficult to read. Most book layout people use a minimum of 11 point font so that those of us with older eyes can see the page better. If you subject is aimed at baby boomers then you are kidding yourself if you think you can go with 10 point type or smaller to save on page count. Most probably won't read it.

You must have a book. Preferably, several books. For a typical non-fiction book you want to limit the total page count to somewhere between 150-225 pages. Go much longer and you start to introduce that factor of overwhelm into the equation again.

You may not be able to include everything you know about a subject in a single book. That is okay. You are better off breaking your knowledge into two or more books if you have enough material then trying to include it all in one and having your book be too long.

Remember, it is all about consumption. If you get them to read your book then the chances of them coming to you for other products and/or services you may offer goes up dramatically.

Always be sure to include in your book several "bounceback" mechanisms. These are ways you can capture the reader's information to follow up with them via autoresponders or offline methods.

When someone buys your book in a traditional retail bookstore or online via Amazon then you do not receive that buyer information. So the inclusion of some bribe inside your book (preferably multiple bribes) to get them to come to your website is important. You can offer some free bonus material or a checklist or anything that they can access only by giving you their contact information.

You must have a book. You must have a book. You must have a book.

Chapter X

EXPANDING YOUR PLATFORM
Coaching, Membership Sites and Products

S peaking is a wonderful thing. It can be a career of its own or you can use it as a tool to build your business. But, if speaking is your core business then you need to make sure you expand your platform.

Why? Because if all you do is deliver keynote presentations then the only time you are influencing people and making money is when you are delivering a presentation. And, if you are a platform speaker who sells from the stage you are only making money when you are pitching from that stage.

Why did you get into speaking in the first place? For most, it is because they have something they know more about than anyone else and they want to share their expertise with others. It might be their own particular motivational story or some specific "how-to" steps to do something.

Whatever your special gift is, the fact that you are reading this book shows you have something you feel you should be sharing with the world. And, if you are like most speakers then you want to positively impact as many people as you can.

So how can you reach people when you are not up on the stage sharing your expertise? You do this by repackaging your content into different formats that can be sold. This could be in the form of products such as books, CD or DVD sets, or Home Study Courses.

It could be in the form of putting your content within a membership site where people pay you monthly to belong to your site where they can access your training materials.

Or it could be in the form of coaching, where you work with either an individual one on one or a group coaching environment where you work with several people simultaneously.

It is all about expanding your reach and whether you consider yourself a speaker first and foremost or you consider yourself a coach who does some speaking or you consider yourself an author or information marketer who speaks to expand your platform it really does not matter. You have your own "Special Sauce" you should be sharing with the world and by expanding your platform you can positively impact a greater number of people.

Most people tend to undervalue the value of the knowledge they have to share. It is tough to make it as a speaker if you are selling nothing but a $20 ebook. You have to sell a lot of $20 ebooks to make any real money.

That is why you need to have a range of products. That $20 ebook can be a great entry product for you. Or your book can fulfill the same role. But you also need to have a $50 product, a $500 product, a $2000 product, a $5000 product and a $10,000 product.

You need products to sell that can generate revenue for you when you are not on the platform. Now the thought of a $5000 or $10,000 product might seem farfetched to you and we recognize that some of you may have an issue with believing you are worth that much.

But you are! If you have specialized knowledge to share that will shortcut someone else's route to success then they will gladly pay you for that shortcut. Do not undervalue the benefits someone can receive by working with you.

If you are a speaker there is only a limited amount that you can teach in a 60 or 90 minute presentation. If you have additional information that you know will benefit your target audience then you are doing a disservice to your market by not making that additional information available to them in some format.

You will have to decide whether that will be via products—physical or digital. Or if it will be via a coaching program(s). Obviously, the higher the ticket price of a coaching program the more direct access to you the members can expect. Or, maybe it will be via a membership site.

Probably it will be some combination of all the above. Some people learn best by reading. Others are auditory learners who would rather listen to you. Some may be more visual where DVDs or online videos would be a better fit. Yet others may be experiential learners who prefer to attend live events.

So what does it all mean? It means the more methodologies in which you can offer up your expertise the wider potential audience you will be able to reach.

The More Methodologies in Which You Can Offer Up Your Expertise the Wider Potential Audience You Can Reach

Now a word of caution here — if you are going to offer coaching programs as part of your product mix. One-on-one coaching can become a tremendous time drain fairly quickly and when you are doing one-on-one coaching you are truly trading your time for dollars. It might be for big dollars, but it is still a time for money trade.

How can you leverage your time to amplify the impact you can have on others? Group coaching is one amplification method, as you now have a one-to-many situation rather than a one-on-one.

You may love coaching and obviously, the decision is ultimately yours as to how much direct access you are going to allow to people who are a member of your coaching program. But we know many speakers who burned out quickly in the one-on-one scenario, so be aware of that going in if you decide that is the route you want to go.

Another way to leverage your time is by putting your content within a membership site. You have to determine at what price point(s) you will offer memberships. If you are going after a mass market audience then a lower price point would probably be more appropriate - $7 to $27 per month. But if your market is a very specific niche market then a higher price point can be commanded. Many coaching programs charge $500 to $1000 per month or more to belong. Again, the higher the price point typically the more amount of direct access to you the members will expect.

Repurposing is a popular topic within the information marketing world and, as a speaker, you definitely need to figure out how many different ways you can repurpose your knowledge for the marketplace. You do not have to reinvent the wheel or start with a blank piece of paper whenever you are creating content. Think about what you already have and how you can utilize it to greater impact.

Sharing your important message with the world is what it is all about. So be sure you expand your platform by sharing your expertise in as many ways as possible.

Products, both in digital and physical formats, membership sites and coaching programs are just some of the ways you can increase your reach. Be sure you incorporate as many of these message "amplifiers" into your speaking business as you are able to over time. Don't expect that you will get it all done overnight. Just keep moving things forward, putting in piece after piece until you have built the speaking empire you want to build.

Chapter Y

YOU

It's All About the Speaker... Or Is It?

n today's meeting, convention and conference environment, this year's event is expected to be better than the last, and everyone from program chairs to professional meeting planners expect every speaker to deliver a polished, captivating presentation. That is only however a small part of what they expect. In this chapter we will explore what else is expected of a speaker who wants to get invited back and how to go beyond expectations so that the person who invited you to speak to is not just a client—instead they are a raving fan.

Recognize everyone talks about the speaker. Meeting planners recount too many stories about speakers who delivered less than their best, were demanding from the moment they arrived, and added stress to the event team's plate.

You want to be a speaker who will create an extraordinary experience for audience members, and add in extras that make whoever hired you look smart, savvy and like a superstar. Do more than "just give a speech."

Become a partner with everyone who books you and deliver incredible results every time both on and off the platform.

Follow these ideas to exceed everyone's expectations, build a reputation of being a team player—not a diva and get invited back over and over.

Be Available

Be the speaker who is available before your presentation and always after your session. It greatly adds to the positive experience attendees have at an event when they can meet the speaker, ask questions, shake hands, pose for a photo, sign books or autographs and visit one-on-one. An exceptional speaker thinks of themselves as a co-host of the event and acts accordingly. This really enhances the attendee experience.

Don't be what is known in the industry as the "hit and run" speaker. We have all seen them—this is the guy or gal who shows up a few minutes before their speech and disappears shortly after their speech has ended—never to be seen again at the event. It leaves a sour taste in the mouths of the attendees and does not ingratiate you with the event promoter.

Be Gracious

Courtesy is always foremost, and speakers need to be able to handle all situations with grace, flexibility and professionalism. It is important that you as the speaker show warmth and be generous with everyone. Do not believe what it says on your speaker marketing materials about you being world-renowned—today you are the hired help, Do not act like a diva, act like a gracious professional.

There will be times when something unexpected happens that is potentially detrimental to your performance on the platform. How you handle yourself when things don't go as expected says a lot about you as a person and how you choose to handle yourself will be noticed by both the event promoter and the audience. Want to kill your future speaking opportunities? Just act like an ass when the going gets bad and you can just about guarantee your failure.

> *"Professionalism: It's NOT the job you DO,*
> *it's HOW you DO the job."*
> —Anonymous

Be a Yes for Last Minute Requests

As the speaker think of yourself as part of the event production team and take on any roles necessary to create a successful experience for the audience. Be willing to handle any activity that arises—if the lunch speaker is delayed you can lead the audience in an exercise until they get there, the auctioneer for the auction does not show up- you can fill in, you are asked to sit with the scholarship recipients for lunch and share with them some of your wisdom. Be a yes for your meeting planner. This makes you a hero and gives you more visibility and another chance to connect with your people.

Don't Wait to Be Asked—Offer

If the emcee for the banquet is sick offer to fill in. If the event planner was planning on passing out plaques from the stage on their own—offer to help. If there is no one to introduce the next breakout session—jump in.

This also means do not wait for someone else to do what needs to be done. I gladly clean up my meeting room when presenting after lunch if the place is untidy. I have moved many chairs, dumped the trash and stacked used drinking glasses. I always chip in and do my part. I do not wait to be asked or find someone else to handle what needs handling. If you become aware of a crisis of any kind—jump in. Be there.

> *"Take your work seriously, but never yourself."*
> —Dame Margot Fonteyn, British prima ballerina

Customize the Presentation

The best speakers provide their clients with a pre-program questionnaire or have a pre-event phone meeting and customize their programs for each event. You never want someone to say you deliver a "canned" speech. Incorporate the theme and objectives of the event into your talk. Depending on the circumstances some speakers interview audience members in advance to get a sense of what they are looking for.

Flexibility is critical as a speaker. If you are going to speak at a multi-speaker event and you find out that another speaker is on the stage before you and is planning to talk about the same thing you were going to cover do you have the ability to change up your presentation in some way to make it different.

A professional speaker finds out what other speakers at an event are going to be covering in advance so they make sure they can deliver uniqueness to the event.

Be Flexible with Technology

Some speakers send a list of their technology needs. Recognize that renting a projector for a PowerPoint presentation can cost a lot for events. Be prepared to bring your own projector or give a presentation without it when your event promoter is on a tight budget.

Always have a backup plan already established for what you will do if the technology breaks down. If your PowerPoint goes ka-bloo-ee what are you going to do? If your clicker doesn't work properly how are you going to handle it? Expect the unexpected and be prepared to handle it.

Help to Generate Pre-Event Excitement

Awesome speakers make themselves available for a pre-conference, tele-seminar or webinar that they deliver for potential attendees. As the speaker, you can also provide videos that you have recorded just for that event. This generates excitement and "buzz" among potential attendees and heightens interest in the event and your presentation. Plus this helps with signups for the event, which means you have a bigger audience.

When you help your event promoter increase attendance and create excitement for the event they will appreciate that and you ensure the success of the event.

Market the Event

Do everything you can to support the marketing efforts of any event you speak at. Provide articles for the promoter to use, add the event to your online calendar, post about the event in your social media effort and of course do a dedicated email to your list if that is appropriate depending on the event. Ask your event promoter what else you can do to support them in marketing their event.

Offer More Value for Later

A smart speaker offers during their talk to send an ebook, valuable list or a audio download that supports the talk to the audience after the talk is over. Even offer to be available for any calls and emails. Having presented to hundreds of audiences of all sizes, I have found that a few participants will call my office after an event with a question. The ones that do so appreciate the attention to their needs and again you are winning with the event promoter.

Stay in touch with audience members who want to hear from you and continue to offer value. This can be a free report, fact sheet, ebook, articles, blog entries and video clips—anything that adds value to the presentation. This type of activity also communicates your ongoing interest in providing value to the group and demonstrates your commitment to serving the group for the long term.

These are ways your can over deliver as a speaker to ensure you create raving fans. When you make your meeting planner's or event promoter's job easier and you make them look good you will be invited back every time.

Don't be a Diva

ZZZZSSS AVOID THEM NODDING OFF

Engage Your Audience and Be a Captivating Speaker Every Time

"Better to be without logic than without emotion."
—Charlotte Bronte, English novelist and poet

So many speakers put all their attention on crafting a great speech when, in fact, a big part of being an awesome presenter is your ability to connect with your audience. Your audience will be open to what you have to say and listen to every word with enthusiasm when they believe you care about them, are there for them and are giving 100% of yourself in the time you are together.

Here are ten audience engagement strategies I use every time I present to engage the audience.

1. Take in The Audience Before You Begin

When you first take the stage, before you begin speaking, take at least 5 seconds to focus on each member of the audience (if they are a small enough group). For larger groups, take a moment to slowly scan the room looking at individuals in each area. Smile at the people you are looking at. Consciously remind yourself that you are here to provide the audience value and serve them, send them some love energy from your heart and feel their interest and support before you begin speaking.

2. Keep Eye Contact

You have heard it said that you have to make eye contact—I am saying you go way beyond that. You keep eye contact. Everything you say is delivered to the eyes of someone in the audience. You do not look at the floor when you walk across the room or stage, you do not glance up to catch a thought, you do not keep talking if you look at your notes. You make sure everything you say is said while you are looking someone in the eyes. This takes practice and it is what separates the captivating speakers from the good speakers.

3. Breathe

Deeply and often; speak in short sentences so you are able to breathe and project easily. Breathe from your diaphragm, take breaths that expand your belly. Deep breathing grounds you in the moment, and draws your listeners to you. My super tip for this, that you will recognize if you have ever sat in my audience, is to ask the audience to take a deep breath, and you take a deep breath with them. This is a unique interactive activity that has them feel more with you.

4. Pause

You need time for your ideas to land, for the audience to reflect on what you have just said, for them to see in their mind the picture of a story you are telling. Do not be afraid of many moments of silence. In fact, embrace them. Pausing is key to holding the attention of the audience. Pauses engage the audience in your talk and serves as a nonverbal underline—that emphasizes your key theme or points. Pausing makes the audience listen more and allows them stay mentally with you.

5. Watch Your Pace

A speech is not a conversation and should not be delivered at the same pace as a conversation. Be aware of how quickly you speak. It is quite common for untrained or inexperienced speakers to talk too fast. Their words blend together and it's hard for the listener to get the meaning of what is being said. One way around this is to focus on speaking more slowly than you normally would in daily conversation. Slower pacing helps your audience understand you better and it adds authority and credibility to your message.

6. Add Vocal Variety

Vocal variety makes your speech more interesting to listen to, it keeps your audience involved. Speak loud enough to be easily heard. The idea is to fill the room with the power of your voice. If you are sharing a funny story, increase your volume when you get to the punch line. Drop to a softer, quieter volume when you want to build suspense or make the audience think you are sharing a secret. Don't use speech fillers: *such as, so, um, ah, ok, um, well,* and *anyway.* These distract the audience and weaken your message.

7. Be Authentic

You can only be yourself. It's good to work with a coach so you master speaking and other business skills—once on the stage it comes down to projecting who you are. We all have a natural truth, and others can see it in us. The reason we are speaking is because we are on a mission. Let that passion shine through. Your audience will forgive speaking blunders if they know we are being genuine, if they can tell we care about them.

8. Be Vulnerable, Don't Always Be The Hero

Your vulnerability draws people to you. It makes your speech more compelling and you more real. Talk about your successes, yes, but also be willing to share a blistering failure and the lesson you learned from that. How you power through your down times is what creates a memorable talk. Our life experiences help others see their own potential, the value they have to bring.

9. Involve the Audience, Keep it Interactive

It's been said that women don't feel they are present at a talk until they hear their own voice. Why not begin with an exercise that gets them talking? Be creative, have them share their compelling vision or the reason why they came to hear you speak. Once they share with each other, ask them to share with the larger group. Keep interacting with the audience throughout your talk. It keeps their interest high and focused on you and your message.

10. Be Yourself, Only Better

Your physical energy: in your body and in your voice is a big part of your delivery and a big part of being captivating. Turn up the volume on your personal energy. If you are normally a four on a scale of one to ten, make that a six in a small group and a ten in a very large group or room. Your energy has to fill the whole room. Vocally you do this with extra enthusiasm or extra excitement in your voice when you are presenting. Always be yourself, and turn up the volume on who you are in front of an audience.

Apply these ideas next time you present and you will find you are better received then before and the audience will be leaning forward in their seats to see what you come up with next. Being a speaker that really engages the audience will have you booked over and over, time and time again.

Being a Speaker that Really Engages the
Audience Will Have You Booked
Over and Over, Time and Time Again

ABOUT THE AUTHORS

Adryenn Ashley   Bret Ridgway   Caterina Rando

Adryenn Ashley

As a mentor to CEOs worldwide, she is directly responsible for adding significant revenue to her client's bottom line. Adryenn founded Wow! Is Me, Inc. after developing a proprietary social media business system that works with both retail and service based businesses. Her elite consulting clients cover a broad spectrum of industries, including motion pictures, food distribution, artificial intelligence and consulting firms. Adryenn earned her 'high tech priestess' stripes by crashing computers and breaking into banks…at their request of course. Now she plus her well-honed techniques to turn fan engagement into #SocialTV profits with CrowdedTV, the ultimate in fan-backed entertainment and the world's first crowdfunding platform for broadcast television shows that goes 2 step further than just raising funds, but also includes sponsorship and distribution.

To receive Adryenn's Free Online Brand Process, go to http://wowisme.net/ABCs

Bret Ridgway

Just a few short years ago you would never have found Bret on stage as a speaker. As co-founder of Speaker Fulfillment Services, a company dedicated to helping speakers, authors and information marketers with the production, warehousing and shipping of their information products, Bret was quite content being a behind-the-scenes guy.

In fact, his company began working with event promoters back in 1999, handling the back-of-the-room sales table at various Internet and information marketing related conferences. As he began working more and more events he got to know a lot of the speakers in the industry. When one of them found out that Bret had founded the first portal website in the plant engineering and maintenance industry, MaintenanceResources.com back in the mid-1990s and was fulfilling tens of thousands of dollars worth of products every month he cornered Bret at an event and asked Bret if he would fulfill some of his products. As a result, Speaker Fulfillment Services was born.

But, after a few more years behind the scenes, Bret recognized he needed to overcome his natural introverted personality and get in the front of the room, just to prove he could do it for himself. And, he did it. Bret is now a frequent presenter on the subject of information marketing at conferences and a frequent guest on webinars, teleseminars and radio shows on the same subject.

In addition to his speaking engagements, Bret is author of multiple books and a co-founder in several business ventures. Besides Speaker Fulfillment Services, Bret is co-founder with Rick Frishman and Bryan Hane of Author101Online.com, a membership site for authors, and co-founder of Disc Delivered and Red Oak Cart.

Caterina Rando

Caterina Rando, MA, MCC, is a business mentor extraordinaire for women speakers, coaches and other entrepreneurs. For over twenty years she has been on a passionate mission to change the world with her brand of economic empowerment that is a combination of running your business with integrity, value-based marketing, staying in action and putting your whole heart in everything you do.

She is a sought after speaker, business success strategist, master certified coach, publisher and author of the national bestselling book *Learn to Power Think* from Chronicle Books.

Caterina has coauthored several books including: *Make Your Connections Count, Incredible Business, Savvy Leadership Strategies for Women, Woman Entrepreneur Extraordinaire, Socially Smart and Savvy,* and *Direct Selling Power.*

Caterina is the founder of the Thriving Women in Business Community and through this organization she and her team conduct a variety of programs designed to provide skills, support and an environment for breakthroughs for women to succeed who want to catapult their businesses to the next level.

Caterina publishes *Thriving Women in Business* magazine, a print and online publication that supports women to take big leaps in their businesses. Get your free subscription at www.twibc.com

She holds a Bachelor of Science in Organizational Behavior and a Master of Arts in Life Transitions Counseling Psychology. She is a Certified Personal and Professional Coach (CPPC) and a Master

Certified Coach (MCC), the highest designation awarded by the International Coaching Federation.

Caterina is an advocate for infusing philanthropy in your business. She is the author of *The Women's Giving Circle Guide: Get Together, Give Together, and Make a Difference,* and founder of the Thriving Women in Business Giving Circle. Find out more about starting your own giving circle at www.twibc.com/givingcircle

ADDITIONAL RESOURCES AVAILABLE FROM YOUR AUTHORS

Adryenn Ashley

To receive Adryenn's Free Online Brand Process, go to http://wowisme.net/ABCs

Bret Ridgway

Services

Speaker Fulfillment Services (SpeakerFulfillmentServices.com) – Provides disc duplication, printing, warehousing and fulfillment services for speakers, authors and information marketers.

Disc Delivered (DiscDelivered.com) – Print on demand self-mailer program for CDs and DVDs perfect for lead generation products or giveaways.

Red Oak Cart (RedOakCart.com) – Robust ecommerce and email system.

Event Materials (MyEventMaterials.com) – Workbooks, badges, lanyards, notepads, pens, bags and all those materials you need for your live events.

Membership Sites

Author 101 Online (Author101Online.com) – On-going training resources for authors about book marketing and publishing.

Books

View from the Back: 101 Tips for Event Promoters Who Want to Dramatically Increase Back-of-the-Room Sales (Available on Amazon.com and at 101TipsForEventPromoters.com)

50 Biggest Mistakes I See Information Marketers Make (Available on Amazon.com)

50 Biggest Website Mistakes Online Business Owners Make: Secrets to Getting More Traffic, Converting More Customers and Making More Sales (With Frank Deardurff – Available on Amazon.com and at 50BiggestWebsiteMistakes.com)

Mistakes Authors Make (Available on Amazon.com and at MistakesAuthorsMake.com)

Consuming Your Content (Available on Amazon.com)

Ebook

The Book on Fulfillment: Questions to Ask Any Potential Fulfillment Partner (With Bryan Hane – Available free at TheBookOnFulfillment.com)

Audio Products

7 Key Concepts You Must Understand as an Information Marketer (With Bryan Hane – Available on Amazon.com)

6 Keys to Building a Successful Info Products Business (With Bryan Hane – Available on Amazon.com)

6 Keys to Standing Out from the Crowd as an Info Marketer (With Bryan Hane – Available on Amazon.com)

6 Keys to Taking Your Info Products Business to the Next Level (With Bryan Hane – Available on Amazon.com)

Looking at Live Events for Speakers and Promoters (With Bryan Hane – Available on Amazon.com)

Running the Online Side of an Info Marketing Business (With Bryan Hane – Available on Amazon.com)

Caterina Rando

Live Events and Coaching Programs

Expand Your Fempire Summit (ExpandYourFempire.com) – This is a two-day live event that provides innovative strategies to grow your revenue and build long-term and lifelong clients while fulfilling your mission and living your ideal life.

The Speak, Sell, Succeed Summit (caterinarando.com/events) – This is a two day live event that shares how to become a sought-after-speaker who knows how to gain insta-clients when you present.

The Thriving Business Platinum Program (www.caterinarando.com/tbpp) – This six month live group program provides comprehensive skill building and guidance designed to grow your revenue while building a profitable and sustainable business.

The Thriving Speaker Platinum Program (www.caterinarando.com/tspp) – This six month live group program provides extensive skill building and guidance on how to build a mid-six figure business with speaking and training as key income streams.

The Thriving Events & Retreats Platinum Program (www.caterinarando.com/terp) – This six month live group program provides resources, checklist, blueprints, marketing strategy and instruction on how to take an idea and turn it into a profitable and ongoing revenue stream as a retreat or event that you do over and over to massively monetize your mastery and grow your business.

Thriving Entrepreneur Elite Mastermind – This is a six month program for women who want to continue to build their fempire, use their business for good and make a big impact through entrepreneurship. Email Caterina if you are interested in finding out more cat@ caterinarando.com.

Breakthrough Luxury Retreat for Women Entrepreneurs (BreakthroughLuxuryRetreat.com) – Caterina knows success comes from the inside out. This event is all about recommitting to your business and identifying blocks interfering with you achieving your goals. This small group event is delivered in a luxury setting that ensures you leave refreshed, rejuvenated and recharged to get busy making your dreams come true.

Audio Products

Sought After Speaker System (www.caterinarando.com/sass) – This proven system is developed by Caterina Rando, MC, MCC. For over twenty years Caterina has been showing women entrepreneurs how to give a speech and come home with insta-clients.

Speaking allows you to showcase your value with many potential clients all at once. Still speaking to gain clients is an art and a science, many people are doing it all wrong. Caterina's proven methods have accelerated the revenue growth of thousands of women entrepreneurs with her easy to implement method. It is your turn.

Influence Power for Women in Business System (www.caterinarando. com/ipsystem) You are ready to build influence in your business. You think you're doing everything that is possible to build and gain more influence with your community and clients. This is a definitive influence building system that will accelerate your business and exciting opportunities to grow your revenue.

Home Study Courses

How to Conduct a Two-Hour Intro Event to Easily Gain Insta-Clients (www.caterinarando.com/how-to-gain-insta-clients/) – This three-hour virtual, intensive is designed for women coaches, consultants, practitioners and speakers. During this info. packed session you gain everything you need to quickly fill your coaching practice or successfully fill your workshops and group programs with two-hour intro events.

Realize Your Events and Retreats Virtual Action Program (www.caterinarando.com/vep) – Is a three month virtual program that is your proven, step-by-step solution to realizing your dream or doing your own programs, of building your own community, of uplifting the lives of other women by gathering them together. This program is filled with little known tips that will save you thousands. You will discover many brilliant ideas that will earn you thousands, this program is for you, the woman who wants to uplift and impact the lives of other women.

A free eBook edition
is available with the
purchase of this book.

To claim your free eBook edition:

1. Download the Shelfie app.
2. Write your name in upper case in the box.
3. Use the Shelfie app to submit a photo.
4. Download your eBook to any device.

Shelfie

A **free** eBook edition is available
with the purchase of this print book.

CLEARLY PRINT YOUR NAME ABOVE IN UPPER CASE

Instructions to claim your free eBook edition:
1. Download the Shelfie app for Android or iOS
2. Write your name in **UPPER CASE** above
3. Use the Shelfie app to submit a photo
4. Download your eBook to any device

Print & Digital Together Forever.

Snap a photo   Free eBook   Read anywhere

The Morgan James Speakers Group

↗ www.TheMorganJamesSpeakersGroup.com

We connect Morgan James published
authors with live and online events
and audiences whom will benefit
from their expertise.

Morgan James makes all of our titles available
through the Library for All Charity Organizations.

www.LibraryForAll.org

9 781683 500124